South Carolina Advanced Real Estate Principles

the S.C.A.P. Unit II Program

2nd Edition

PERFORMANCE
PROGRAMS
COMPANY

Stephen Mettling
David Cusic
Ryan Mettling

Material in this book is not intended to represent legal advice and should not be so construed. Readers should consult legal counsel for advice regarding points of law.

© 2024 by Performance Programs Company
6810 190th Street East, Bradenton, FL 34211
info@performanceprogramscompany.com
www.performanceprogramscompany.com

ISBN: 978-1965482001

South Carolina Advanced Real Estate Principles: the S.C.A.P. Unit II Program

Table of Contents

South Carolina Advanced Real Estate Principles (Unit II)

Course Overview

The South Carolina Advanced Real Estate Principles (the "SCAP" Unit II Program) has been developed to satisfy South Carolina's 30-hour Unit II requirement. The course also fulfills the Real Estate Commission's objective of giving South Carolina real estate licensees a carefully developed reinforcement of key real estate brokerage principles, concepts, and practices necessary to initiate a productive, professional career in real estate.

Beyond an initial review of key principles, the SCAP Program takes on a further examination of essential skills and practices that will be necessary to meet client and customer transactional requirements within South Carolina's legal framework. Such skills examined include compliance with South Carolina agency and disclosure laws; how to properly represent and disclose property characteristics; and an intensive look at South Carolina transaction contracts: listings; the sales contract; options and contracts for deed. Beyond its agency and contracts topics, the SCAP further examines the other key subjects required by the Commission: ethics; handling trust funds; regulatory compliance; and critical cornerstones of professional practice. Finally, the last two modules of the SCAP program examine the various methods used to measure real property; price and appraise real property; and evaluate how real property is evaluated as a professional investment. These considerations encompass income properties as well as residential non-income property, and include pre-tax analysis as well as after-tax analysis.

Taken as a whole, the South Carolina Advanced Real Estate Principles program is designed to deepen the new licensee's understanding of how brokerage works in actual practice – and how it is supposed to be undertaken in view of today's standards of professionalism, ethics, and legal compliance.

ABOUT THE AUTHORS

Stephen Mettling. For nearly fifty years, Stephen Mettling has been actively engaged in real estate education. Beginning with Dearborn in 1972, then called Real Estate Education Company, Mr. Mettling managed the company's textbook division and author acquisitions. Subsequently he built up the company's real estate school division which eventually became the country's largest real estate, insurance and securities school network in the country. In 1978, Mr. Mettling founded Performance Programs Company, a custom training program publishing and development company specializing in commercial, industrial, and corporate real estate. Over time, Performance Programs Company narrowed its focus to real estate textbook and exam prep publishing. Currently the Company's texts and prelicense resources are used in hundreds of schools in over 48 states. As of 2022, Mr. Mettling has authored over 100 textbooks, real estate programs and exam prep manuals.

David Cusic, Ph.D. Dr. Cusic has been a training consultant, author, and Performance Programs Company partner for over forty years. As an educator with international real estate training experience, Dr. Cusic has been engaged in vocation-oriented education since 1966. Specializing in real estate training since 1983, he has developed numerous real estate training programs for corporate and institutional clients nationwide. Dr. Cusic is co-author of the Company's flagship title, Principles of Real Estate Practice by Mettling and Cusic, now complemented by over 20 state supplements and 30+ exam prep texts.

Ryan Mettling. Ryan Mettling, partner and currently publisher of Performance Programs, is an accomplished online curriculum designer, author and course developer.

KEY CONTRIBUTOR

Kseniya Korneva. Kseniya Korneva is a licensed REALTOR® in Tampa, Florida with a passion for writing and editing. She graduated with a Civil Engineering degree from Clemson University and fell in love with real estate shortly after. Coming from a long line of academics, her love for education runs deep. Kseniya was first introduced to the world of publishing after writing her own ebook in 2019 and realized she wanted to dive deeper. In her free time, she loves to write about personal finance and real estate on her blog (www.TheMoneyMinimalists.com).

Module A: Agency and Property Disclosure

Unit 1: Agency
Unit 2: Property Disclosure
Unit 3: Other Brokerage Disclosures

Module A Learning Objectives

Agency

> 1. Describe the purpose and essential provisions of South Carolina brokerage agreements and transaction contracts

> 2. Describe the general process and pitfalls to avoid in completing a listing agreement or sale contract

> 3. Summarize the content, proper timing, and acknowledgements required to properly disclose one's agency relationship

Property Disclosure

> 1. Describe what must be included in proper, thorough property disclosures

> 2. Summarize the licensee's and the client's responsibilities in completing the seller's property condition disclosure form

> 3. Describe how the buyer's right of rescission works with respect to property condition disclosure

Other Brokerage Disclosures

> 1. Characterize the licensee's disclosure duties with respect to selling one's own property, selling stigmatized property, selling property as-is, and Megan's Law

Unit 1: AGENCY

Unit 1: Agency - Learning Objectives

When the student has completed Unit 1, he or she will be able to:

1. Describe the purpose and essential provisions of South Carolina brokerage agreements and transaction contracts

2. Describe the general process and pitfalls to avoid in completing a listing agreement or sale contract

3. Summarize the content, proper timing, and acknowledgements required to properly disclose one's agency relationship

BROKERAGE AGREEMENTS IN SOUTH CAROLINA

Listing contracts

A listing contract is an agreement between a broker and a seller, authorizing the broker to perform the services stated in the agreement for a fee.

The South Carolina Real Estate Commission requires that certain language be used in all South Carolina listing contracts as of January 2017. The required language is as follows:

Seller acknowledges receiving an explanation of the types of agency relationships that are offered by brokerage and a South Carolina Disclosure of Real Estate Brokerage Relationships form at the first practical opportunity at which substantive contact occurred between the agent and seller.

*Seller acknowledges that after entering into this written agency contract, agent might request a modification in order to act as a **dual agent** or a **designated agent** in a specific transaction. If asked:*

- *permission to act as a dual agent will not be considered.*
- *permission to act as a dual agent may be considered at the time I am provided with information about the other party to a transaction. If I agree, I will execute a separate written Dual Agency Agreement.*
- *permission to act as a designated agent will not be considered.*
- *permission to act as a designated agent may be considered at the time I am provided with information about the other party to a transaction. If I agree, I will execute a separate written **Designated Agency Agreement.***

Key listing contract provisions

Listing contracts in South Carolina contain a number of provisions, as follows.

Consent to disclosed dual agency/designated agency. South Carolina requires specific language be adopted in this section, and the seller must initial all applicable choices.

Compensation to other agents. The owner authorizes the broker to cooperate and pay compensation to other agents. If there will be no compensation to other agents, the property cannot be listed in the multiple listing service.

Terms. The agreed upon listing price is recorded in this section along with the compensation the broker will receive.

Earnest money. The buyer authorizes and designates an escrow agent to hold the earnest money deposit.

Signs. Owner gives permission for the display of signs on the property, relating to its sale.

Broker's duty. Broker agrees to best efforts of agents and staff in procuring a buyer.

Broker liability limitation. This provision explains the limits of the broker's liability to the owner with regard to acts of omission, negligence, misrepresentation, or breach of undertaking, except if the acts were intentional or willful.

Owners' duty. This section lists the owner's obligations to the broker, including such items as furnishing complete and reliable information, allowing inspections and property showings, permitting the broker to take photographs, conveying marketable title to the property, and authorizing the attorneys to provide a copy of the settlement statement to the broker prior to closing.

Property disclosure statement. Owner warrants that there are no material defects that have not been disclosed and that the owner has reviewed and completed a Seller's Property Disclosure Statement.

Disclosure. Broker is authorized to disclose information about the property to agents, subagents, and prospective buyers.

Taxes. Owner agrees to comply with South Carolina withholding requirements for nonresident owners.

Coastal Tidelands & Wetlands Act. Statement that an addendum will be attached if the property is affected by the provisions of this Act.

Multiple listing service. This section indicates whether or not the property will be listed with a multiple listing service.

Lockbox. The owner agrees to lockbox installation or not.

Internet marketing. The owner agrees that the listing may be placed in electronic marketing media or not.

Other offers. The broker's responsibility to present offers ends at the property's closing or at the expiration of the listing agreement.

Marketing the property. The broker will end marketing efforts once an offer has been accepted, unless requested to continue in writing.

No control of commission rates or fees. Compensation for services is negotiated between broker and client and is not controlled, recommended, suggested or maintained by a Board, MLS, or any person not a party to the listing agreement.

Maintenance. Owner will maintain the property until date of closing or possession.

Agreement to sell. Owner agrees to enter into a written sales agreement with a buyer.

Lead-based paint. Appropriate disclosure will be signed and attached to the agreement for any property with a dwelling built before 1978.

Mediation clause. Any dispute or claim resulting from a breach of the agreement or services provided will go to mediation. This clause survives for 120 days after the closing date.

Fair housing. Property is offered in full compliance with fair housing laws.

Facsimile. The agreement may be communicated by fax or other electronic means and all initials and signatures are valid and binding.

Enforcement. Broker may take action to enforce the agreement or collect costs, fees, and damages.

Sex offender/criminal information. Broker is not responsible for getting or disclosing such information. Seller may obtain such information from local law enforcement.

Signature block. This section contains spaces for owners, witnesses, and licensee to sign.

Buyer representation contracts

The South Carolina Real Estate Commission also requires that certain language be used in all South Carolina buyer representation contracts. The required language is as follows:

> *Buyer acknowledges receiving an explanation of the types of agency relationships that are offered by brokerage and a South Carolina Disclosure of Real Estate Brokerage Relationships form at the first practical opportunity at which substantive contact occurred between the agent and seller.*
>
> *Buyer acknowledges that after entering into this written agency contract, agent might request a modification in order to act as **a dual agent** or a **designated agent** in a specific transaction. If asked:*
>
> > * *permission to act as a dual agent will not be considered.*
> >
> > * *permission to act as a dual agent may be considered at the time I am provided with information about the other party to a*

transaction. If I agree, I will execute a separate written Dual Agency Agreement.

- *permission to act as a designated agent will not be considered.*
- *permission to act as a designated agent may be considered at the time I am provided with information about the other party to a transaction. If I agree, I will execute a separate written Designated Agency Agreement.*

Buyer representation contracts in South Carolina contain a number of provisions, as follows.

Appointment of broker. The buyer's name and the broker's name are written into this paragraph.

Purpose of agency. This section indicates the type of property and terms the buyer is seeking.

Broker's duties. The broker agrees to use professional skills and knowledge to represent the buyer and to locate an appropriate property that is available and suitable.

Buyer's duties. This section lists the buyer's obligations to the broker, including the agreement to work exclusively with this broker and its affiliated licensees during the term of the agreement, to provide reliable financial information to the broker, and to provide the requirements for the type of property the buyer is seeking, along with price range and other terms.

Compensation. The buyer can choose, by checking the appropriate sections, whether the buyer will pay the broker a retainer fee, a service fee, and/or a brokerage fee or whether the broker will receive compensation as a cooperating broker from the listing broker.

Term of agency. This section states the beginning and ending date of the agreement.

Consent to disclosed dual agency/designated agency. As mentioned earlier, South Carolina requires specific language in this section and the buyer must initial all applicable choices.

Other potential buyers. Buyer gives consent for the broker to work with other potential buyers who may have similar buyer representation agreements with the broker.

Indemnification of broker. Buyer must tell broker about signing an agency agreement with another broker, or being given information by another broker about a property that is the subject of a contract. If buyer fails to tell broker about another broker's involvement, buyer may be liable to pay broker for any losses or damages resulting from a claim brought against him.

Disclosure of buyer's identity/confidentiality. This section indicates whether or not the broker has the buyer's permission to disclose buyer's identity to other parties.

Broker liability limitation. This provision explains the limits of the broker's liability to the buyer with regard to acts of omission, negligence, misrepresentation, or breach of undertaking, except if the acts were intentional or willful.

Nondiscrimination. All actions carried out under the contract are in full compliance with fair housing laws.

Professional counsel. Buyer acknowledges that broker is retained as a real estate professional and not an attorney.

Mediation clause. Any dispute or claim resulting from a breach of the agreement or services provided will go to mediation. This clause survives for 120 days after the closing date.

Sex offender/criminal information. Broker is not responsible for getting or disclosing such information. Buyer may obtain such information from local law enforcement.

Entire binding agreement. Terms and conditions of agreement are binding and can only be changed by a written agreement signed by both parties.

Facsimile and other electronic means. The agreement may be communicated by fax or other electronic means and all initials and signatures are valid and binding.

Signature block. This section contains spaces for buyers and licensee to sign.

Transaction broker agreements

As with a listing contract and a buyer representation contract, the South Carolina Real Estate Commission requires that certain language be used in all transaction broker agreements entered into with a customer. The required language is as follows:

> *Customer agrees that Transaction Broker is not an agent of the Customer, Customer has not established a client relationship with the Transaction Broker, and the Transaction Broker is not acting in a fiduciary capacity.*
>
> *Customer agrees that Transaction Broker is not an advocate for the interests of Customer.*
>
> *Customer agrees that Transaction Broker will act under limited confidentiality and will not disclose:*

> - *if Customer is the buyer, information concerning Customer's motivation to buy or willingness to make a higher offer than the price submitted on a written offer.*
> - *if Customer is the seller, factors motivating the Customer to sell or willingness to accept an offer less than list price.*
> - *that Customer as a seller or buyer will agree to financing terms other than those offered.*
> - *information requested by Customer to remain confidential, except information required by law to be disclosed.*

The language quoted above dealing with limited confidentiality is not required if the customer waives limited confidentiality in writing.

Also, the transaction broker agreement must include the term of the agreement, a description of the services the licensee will provide to the customer, and the compensation (if any) the transaction broker will receive for providing the services.

SOUTH CAROLINA AGENCY DISCLOSURE

South Carolina permits a licensee to establish the following agency relationships:

- single agency (either with a seller or a buyer)
- disclosed dual agency
- designated agency
- transaction brokerage

It is important that all potential buyers and sellers clearly understand the possible brokerage relationships that can exist and how each relationship changes the role and duties the broker owes to the customer or client. Moreover, many consumers are not aware that real estate agency relationships are with a broker, not a specific licensee.

South Carolina license law requires licensees to explain to real estate consumers the information regarding brokerage relationships at the licensee's firm. In order to meet this requirement, licensees must present consumers with the Commission-approved *South Carolina Disclosure of Real Estate Brokerage Relationships* form, as follows.

SOUTH CAROLINA DISCLOSURE OF REAL ESTATE BROKERAGE RELATIONSHIPS

South Carolina Real Estate Commission
PO BOX 11847, Columbia, S.C. 29211-1847
Telephone: (803) 896-4400   Fax: (803) 896-4427
http://llr.sc.gov/POL/REC/

Pursuant to South Carolina Real Estate License Law in S.C. Code of Laws Section 40-57-370, a real estate licensee is required to provide you a meaningful explanation of agency relationships offered by the licensee's brokerage firm. This must be done at the first practical opportunity when you and the licensee have substantive contact.

Before you begin to work with a real estate licensee, it is important for you to know the difference between a broker-in-charge and associated licensees. The broker-in-charge is the person in charge of a real estate brokerage firm. Associated licensees may work only through a broker-in-charge. In other words, when you choose to work with any real estate licensee, your business relationship is legally with the brokerage firm and not with the associated licensee.

A real estate brokerage firm and its associated licensees can provide buyers and sellers valuable real estate services, whether in the form of basic customer services, or through client-level agency representation. The services you can expect will depend upon the legal relationship you establish with the brokerage firm. It is important for you to discuss the following information with the real estate licensee and agree on whether in your business relationship you will be a customer or a client.

You Are a Customer of the Brokerage Firm

South Carolina license law defines customers as buyers or sellers who choose NOT to establish an agency relationship. The law requires real estate licensees to perform the following *basic duties* when dealing with *any* real estate buyer or seller as customers: *present all offers in a timely manner, account for money or other property received on your behalf, provide an explanation of the scope of services to be provided, be fair and honest and provide accurate information, provide limited confidentiality, and disclose "material adverse facts" about the property or the transaction which are within the licensee's knowledge.*

Unless or until you enter into a written agreement with the brokerage firm for agency representation, you are considered a "customer" of the brokerage firm, and the brokerage firm will not act as your agent. As a customer, you should not expect the brokerage firm or its licensees to promote your best interest.

Customer service does not require a written agreement; therefore, you are not committed to the brokerage firm in any way unless a transaction broker agreement or compensation agreement obligates you otherwise.

Transaction Brokerage

A real estate brokerage firm may offer transaction brokerage in accordance with S.C. Code of Laws Section 40-57-350. Transaction broker means a real estate brokerage firm that provides customer service to a buyer, a seller, or both in a real estate transaction. A transaction broker may be a single agent of a party in a transaction giving the other party customer service. A transaction broker also may facilitate a transaction without representing either party. The duties of a brokerage firm offering transaction brokerage relationship to a customer can be found in S.C. Code of Laws Section 40-57-350(L)(2).

You Can Become a Client of the Brokerage Firm

Clients receive more services than customers. If client status is offered by the real estate brokerage firm, you can become a client by entering into a written agency agreement requiring the brokerage firm and its associated licensees to act as an agent on your behalf and promote your best interests. If you choose to become a client, you will be asked to confirm in your written representation agreement that you received this agency relationships disclosure document in a timely manner.

A *seller becomes a client* of a real estate brokerage firm by signing a formal listing agreement with the brokerage firm. For a seller to become a client, this agreement must be in writing and must clearly establish the terms of the agreement and the obligations of both the seller and the brokerage firm which becomes the agent for the seller.

A *buyer becomes a client* of a real estate brokerage firm by signing a formal buyer agency agreement with the brokerage firm. For a buyer to become a client, this agreement must be in writing and must clearly establish the terms of the agreement and the obligations of both the buyer and the brokerage firm which becomes the agent for the buyer.

(Rev 1/17) Page 1 of 2

14

SOUTH CAROLINA DISCLOSURE OF REAL ESTATE BROKERAGE RELATIONSHIPS

LLR
sc.gov

South Carolina Real Estate Commission
PO BOX 11847, Columbia, S.C. 29211-1847
Telephone: (803) 896-4400   Fax: (803) 896-4427
http://llr.sc.gov/POL/REC/

If you enter into a written agency agreement, as a client, the real estate brokerage has the following *client-level duties: obedience, loyalty, disclosure, confidentiality, accounting, and reasonable skill and care*. Client-level services also include advice, counsel and assistance in negotiations.

Single Agency

When the brokerage firm represents only one client in the same transaction (the seller or the buyer), it is called single agency.

Dual Agency

Dual agency exists when the real estate brokerage firm has two clients in one transaction – a seller client and a buyer client. At the time you sign an agency agreement, you may be asked to acknowledge whether you would consider giving written consent allowing the brokerage firm to represent both you and the other client in a disclosed dual agency relationship.

Disclosed Dual Agency

In a disclosed dual agency, the brokerage firm's representation duties are limited because the buyer and seller have recognized conflicts of interest. Both clients' interests are represented by the brokerage firm. As a disclosed dual agent, the brokerage firm and its associated licensees cannot advocate on behalf of one client over the other, and cannot disclose confidential client information concerning the price negotiations, terms, or factors motivating the buyer/client to buy or the seller/client to sell. Each Dual Agency Agreement contains the names of both the seller client(s) and the buyer client(s) and identifies the property.

Designated Agency

In designated agency, a broker-in-charge may designate individual associated licensees to act solely on behalf of each client. Designated agents are not limited by the brokerage firm's agency relationship with the other client, but instead have a duty to promote the best interest of their clients, including negotiating a price. The broker-in-charge remains a disclosed dual agent for both clients, and ensures the assigned agents fulfill their duties to their respective clients. At the time you sign an agency agreement, you may be asked to acknowledge whether you would consider giving written consent allowing the brokerage firm to designate a representative for you and one for the other client in a designated agency. Each Designated Agency Agreement contains the names of both the seller client(s) and the buyer client(s) and identifies the property.

It's Your Choice

As a real estate consumer in South Carolina, it is your choice as to the type and nature of services you receive.

- You can choose to remain a customer and represent yourself, with or without a transaction broker agreement.
- You can choose to hire the brokerage firm for representation through a written agency agreement.
- If represented by the brokerage firm, you can decide whether to go forward under the shared services of dual agency or designated agency or to remain in single agency.

If you plan to become a client of a brokerage firm, the licensee will explain the agreement to you fully and answer questions you may have about the agreement. Remember, however that until you enter into a representation agreement with the brokerage firm, you are considered a customer and the brokerage firm cannot be your advocate, cannot advise you on price or terms, and only provides limited confidentiality unless a transaction broker agreement obligates the brokerage firm otherwise.

The choice of services belongs to you – the South Carolina real estate consumer.

Acknowledgement of Receipt by Consumer:

Signature _____   Date _____

Signature _____   Date _____

THIS DOCUMENT IS NOT A CONTRACT.
This brochure has been approved by South Carolina Real Estate Commission for use in explaining representation issues in real estate transactions and consumer rights as a buyer or seller. Reprinting without permission is permitted provided no changes or modifications are made.

(Rev 1/17) Page **2** of **2**

Timing

South Carolina presumes that at the time of a licensee's first substantive contact with a potential buyer or seller, that individual is a customer of the real estate brokerage. In this role, the real estate brokerage will be acting as a transaction broker. While acting as a transaction broker, the real estate brokerage and its affiliated licensees can offer services to the customer until the potential buyer or seller signs an agency representation agreement.

According to the legislation, the definition of "substantive contact" is the following: "Contact in which a discussion or dialogue between the consumer and the supervised licensee moves from casual introductory talk to a meaningful conversation regarding the selling or buying motives or objectives of the seller or buyer, financial qualifications, and other confidential information that if disclosed could harm the consumer's bargaining position."

The law says that at the first practical opportunity after substantive contact with potential buyers or sellers, the licensee must

- give the customer the South Carolina Disclosure of Real Estate Brokerage Relationships form and answer any questions the customer might have regarding the form's contents.
- provide a meaningful explanation of the various brokerage relationships the licensee's real estate brokerage offers, including how each relationship affects customer and client services provided.

First substantive contact can occur in person, over the phone, through email, and through other electronic means. Therefore, a licensee can send the form electronically in order to adhere to the requirements for delivery.

Since the form must be provided at the first practical opportunity, it should be delivered to and signed by the consumer before entering into any agency agreement and before writing or presenting a purchase agreement.

Informed consent

The disclosure form requires the signature of the potential buyer or seller. This signature provides an acknowledgment of receipt of the disclosure form and an understanding of the form's contents.

The customer should sign the form after understanding the customer's rights with regard to relationships with real estate brokerages. This includes knowing the possible relationships that could exist between the customer and the broker, and understanding how different relationships allow the broker and associate licensees to provide different levels of service.

The licensee must include the signed copy of the South Carolina Disclosure of Real Estate Brokerage Relationships form in any subsequent agency agreement between the brokerage and the customer. In addition, each sales contract requires both the buyer and the seller to acknowledge if they received customer or client service in the transaction.

SNAPSHOT REVIEW:

Unit 1: AGENCY

BROKERAGE AGREEMENTS IN SOUTH CAROLINA
Listing contract

- agreement between broker and seller authorizing broker to perform services stated in agreement for fee
- **Consent to disclosed dual agency/designated agency.** Agent might request modification to act as dual or designated agent; seller initial acknowledgement
- **Compensation to agents.** Owner authorizes broker to pay compensation to other agents
- **Terms.** Listing price and broker compensation
- **Earnest money.** Buyer designates escrow agent
- **Signs.** Owner gives permission to display signs
- **Broker's duty.** Broker makes best effort to procure buyer
- **Broker liability limitation.** Limits broker liability to owner for omission, negligence, misrepresentation, breach of undertaking
- **Owners' duty.** Owner's obligations to broker
- **Property disclosure statement.** Owner warrants that no material defects exist
- **Disclosure.** Broker authorized to disclose information to agents, subagents, buyers
- **Taxes.** Owner complies with SC withholding requirements
- **Coastal Tidelands & Wetlands Act.** Addendum included if property affected by provisions of Act
- **Multiple listing service.** Whether property in MLS
- **Lockbox.** Owner agrees to lockbox
- **Internet marketing.** Owner agrees to electronic marketing
- **Other offers.** Broker requirement to present offers ends at closing or listing agreement expiration
- **Marketing property.** Broker ends marketing efforts with accepted offer
- **No control of commission rates or fees.** Compensation negotiated between broker and client
- **Maintenance.** Owner maintains property until closing
- **Agreement to sell.** Written sales agreement between owner and buyer
- **Lead-based paint.** Disclosure signed if property built before 1978
- **Mediation clause.** Disputes go into mediation
- **Fair housing.** Property in full compliance with fair housing laws
- **Facsimile.** Agreement by fax or electronic means possible
- **Enforcement.** Broker may enforce agreement or collect costs, fees, damages
- **Sex offender/criminal information.** Broker not responsible for disclosing
- **Signature block.** Owners, witnesses, licensee sign

Buyer representation contract

- agreement between broker and buyer
- agent might request modification to act as dual or designated agent
- **Appointment of broker.** Buyer and broker name

- **Purpose of agency.** Type of property and terms buyer seeking
- **Broker's duties.** Professional skills and knowledge to represent buyer and locate property
- **Buyer's duties.** Work exclusively with broker
- **Compensation.** Buyer chooses to pay retainer, service, brokerage fee
- **Term of agency.** Length of agreement
- **Consent.** To disclosed dual/designated agency
- **Other potential buyers.** Buyer gives consent for broker to work with other similar buyers
- **Indemnification of broker.** Buyer must tell broker about any other agency agreements
- **Disclosure of buyer's identity/confidentiality.** Whether broker can disclose buyer's identity
- **Broker liability limitation.** Limits of broker's liability to buyer regarding omission, negligence, misrepresentation, breach of undertaking
- **Nondiscrimination.** Actions comply with fair housing laws
- **Professional counsel.** Broker is not attorney
- **Mediation clause.** Disputes go into mediation
- **Sex offender/criminal information.** Broker not responsible for disclosing
- **Entire binding agreement.** Terms and conditions are binding
- **Facsimile and other electronic means.** Agreement by fax or electronic means possible
- **Signature block.** Owners, witnesses, licensee sign

Transaction broker agreements

- must include term of agreement, description of services, compensation

SOUTH CAROLINA AGENCY DISCLOSURE

- single agency; disclosed dual agency; designated agency; transaction brokerage

Timing

- first substantive contact with potential client assumes individual is a customer and brokerage acting as transaction brokerage
- licensee must give customer the South Carolina Disclosure of Real Estate Brokerage Relationships form and explain them at first practical opportunity

Informed consent

- buyer or seller must sign disclosure form

==

Check Your Understanding Quiz:

Unit 1: Agency

Carefully read each question and provide your best answer based on what you learned in this module. Then check your answers against the Answer Key which immediately follows the quiz questions.

1. Compensation for brokerage services is _____.

   a. determined by the MLS.
   b. negotiated between broker and client.
   c. controlled by the National Board.
   d. recommended by the local government.

2. In the context of transaction disclosures, a broker is NOT responsible for obtaining _____.

   a. sex offender information.
   b. a signed lead-based paint disclosure.
   c. an executed listing agreement.
   d. a signed Coastal Tidelands & Wetlands Act addendum.

3. Licensees must present consumers with the _____.

   a. South Carolina Disclosure of Real Estate Brokerage Relationships form.
   b. Commission Disclosure form.
   c. Informed Consent form.
   d. Real Estate Sales form.

4. Which type of agreement allows a broker to act in limited confidentiality and forego any fiduciary duties?

   a. Buyer representation contract
   b. Listing contract
   c. Transaction brokerage agreement
   d. Licensee designation agreement

5. If a listing agreement does not provide for any compensation to other agents, then _____.

   a. the property acts as a for-sale-by-owner listing.
   b. the home can be listed in the MLS and buyer's agents must negotiate for their commission.
   c. the standard 3% commission is granted to the buyer's agent.
   d. the property cannot be listed in the MLS.

6. A compliant lead-based paint disclosure must be signed for any property built before _____.

   a. 1978.
   b. 1950.
   c. 1899.
   d. 1989.

7. The buyer representation contract provides for handling disputes or breaches of the contract via which of the following contract-dispute resolution methods?

   a. Professional counseling
   b. Mediation
   c. Indemnification
   d. Interpleader action

8. Which of the following is an owner's obligation to the broker?

   a. Putting a lockbox on the property
   b. Ordering a yard sign for marketing
   c. Procuring a buyer
   d. Conveying marketable title to the property

9. Who decides on the selection of an escrow agent?

   a. The owner's appraiser
   b. The buyer
   c. The listing agent
   d. The buyer's agent

10. What form is a seller required to acknowledge in order for an agent to act as a designated agent?

   a. Transaction Brokerage Agreement
   b. Double Party Agreement
   c. Designated Agency Agreement
   d. Dual Listing Agency Agreement

===

Exercise Workshop -- Unit 1: Agency

Exercise 1-1. Agency Disclosure

Synopsis:

This exercise will identify the duties required in the different forms of agency as well as what South Carolina contracts are used to initiate and legalize these relationships.

Instructions:

1. Determine the type of agency relationship described in the four scenarios given. Then identify the contracts you would use in the given scenario.
2. Each question may have multiple answers.

Activity:

Agency Relationships:

A. Single Agent
B. Duel Agent
C. Transaction Broker
D. Designated Agent

Contracts:

R. Listing Agreement
S. Buyer Brokerage Agreement
T. Transaction Broker Agreement
U. Disclosure of Agency Relationship

1. Mary and Lou want to sell their home and move into a retirement community. They invite Broker Janet to come to their home to give them advice on how to proceed. Janet presents her finding of a CMA she prepared for their meeting. Mary and Lou agree to list their home with Janet. They request that the brokerage only represent them in the transaction.

   _____ What type of agency relationship are Lou and Mary requesting?

   _____ Which contracts and or documents should Janet give her new clients?

2. Broker JoAnn has a listing on a house. She also has a buyer whom she believes would love the house. She wants to make sure that each of these clients is well represented in the transaction. She assigns the seller to one agent in her office and another agent to the buyer. They will each represent their client to the best of their ability. Broker JoAnn will only work as a consultant on any negotiations.

   _____ What type of agency relations is Broker JoAnn setting up?

   _____ What contracts or documents should the agents give their clients?

3. Broker Leslie has a house listed. She also has a client she suspects would be interested in purchasing the property. She is going to represent both the buyer and the seller in the same transaction.

_____ What type of agency relationship is Broker Lesile in?

_____ What contracts or documents should Broker Leslie give to her clients?

4. Bob asks Broker John to help him fill out a contract for the sale of Bob's home. Bob has already found a buyer and has negotiated the sale. Broker John will not be an agent of Bob.

_____ What type of agency relationship do Bob and Broker John have?

_____ What contracts or documents should Broker John give to Bob?

Unit 2: Property Disclosure

Unit 2: Property Disclosure – Learning Objectives

When the student has completed Unit 2, he or she will be able to:

1. Describe what must be included in proper, thorough property disclosures

2. Summarize the licensee's and the client's responsibilities in completing the seller's property condition disclosure form

3. Describe how the buyer's right of rescission works with respect to property condition disclosure

---

PROPERTY CONDITION AND MATERIAL FACTS

Duty to inform

An agent has the duty to inform the client of all material facts, reports, and rumors that might affect the client's interests in the property transaction. A material fact is one that might affect the value or desirability of the property to a buyer if the buyer knew it. Material facts include

- the agent's opinion of the property's condition
- adverse facts about property condition, title defects, environmental hazards, and property defects

In recent years, the disclosure standard has been raised to require an agent to disclose items that a practicing agent should know, whether the agent actually had the knowledge or not, and regardless of whether the disclosure furthers or impedes the progress of the transaction.

Facts not considered to be material, and therefore not usually subject to required disclosure, include such items as property stigmatization (e.g., that a crime or death occurred on the property) and the presence of registered sex offenders in the neighborhood (in accordance with Megan's Law, federal legislation that requires convicted offenders to register with the state of residence; in some states, agents must provide registry information to buyers).

The agent may be held liable for failing to disclose a material fact if a court rules that the typical agent in that area would detect and recognize the adverse condition. There is no obligation to obtain or disclose information that is immaterial to the transaction, such as property stigmas.

Red flag issues

An agent who sees a "red flag" issue such as a potential structural or mechanical problem should advise the seller to seek expert advice. Red flags can seriously impact the value of the property and/or the cost of remediation. In addition to property condition per se, they may include such things as

- environmental concerns
- property anomalies, such as over-sized or peculiarly shaped lot
- neighborhood issues
- poor construction
- signs of flooding
- poor floorplan
- adjacent property features

ENVIRONMENTAL HAZARDS

Health hazards represent a significant disclosure challenge for real estate licensees as they can constitute material facts that affect a principal's decision to complete a transaction. For this reason, licensees should be aware of those hazards which should be detected and disclosed during the process of contracting and closing a conveyance transaction.

Health hazards occur within structures, on real estate parcels, and in the area surrounding real estate. They may occur naturally or as a result of human activity. Environmental laws regulate some, but not all, health hazards that affect real estate.

Specific environmental hazards and issues

Lead-based paint. This hazard cannot be absorbed through the skin, but it becomes dangerous when it is ingested or inhaled. It can be found in most homes built before 1978 and can be present in the air, drinking water, food, contaminated soil, deteriorating paint, and dust from the paint. Children are particularly susceptible because young children are known to eat chips of the paint, allowing the lead to enter their bloodstreams. Homebuyers and renters are required to be given the EPA-HUD-US Consumer Product Safety Commission's booklet, "Protect Your Family from Lead in Your Home" and must be informed if lead-based paint is present in the home. Buyers may have a risk assessment performed prior to purchasing the home.

Mold. This is a fungus that grows under moist conditions and causes allergic reaction for some people. The presence of mold in the home must be disclosed as a latent defect. Flooding and water damage must also be disclosed as both of those can lead to mold growth. Inspections do not always find mold because it often grows inside walls and ductwork. Most molds require removal by a professional.

Asbestos. While harmless in its original condition, it can cause lung cancer if its dust filters into the air. If it is found in a home during remodeling, it must be removed by professionals to prevent contamination. It can be found in roofing and siding, older insulation, textured paint, artificial ashes sold for gas fireplaces, some vinyl floor tiles, coatings for older hot water and steam pipes.

Air quality. The quality of air in a home can be adversely impacted by the presence of carbon monoxide, radon, deteriorating asbestos and lead-based paint, methamphetamine production, formaldehyde, and other toxic chemicals. Homes can and should be tested for many of these contaminants prior to purchase.

Water quality. Ground water is easily contaminated from septic tanks, agricultural runoff, highway de-icing, landfills, pesticides, animal waste, etc. Many people rely on ground water for drinking so must be aware that contaminated water can cause problems from mild stomach problems to cancer and death. The Environmental Protection Agency (EPA) sets standards for protecting ground water from contamination. It also offers advice and resources to facilitate the rehabilitation of contaminated ground water sources. One such means of protection is to advise private well users to have the water tested at least once a year.

Carbon monoxide. This is an odorless, colorless, toxic gas that can kill a person before its presence is known. It can be caused by unvented kerosene and gas space heaters; leaking chimneys; back-drafting from furnaces, gas water heaters, wood stoves, and fireplaces; gas stoves, gasoline powered equipment, vehicle exhaust in garages, tobacco smoke. Carbon monoxide can be detected in a structure by a unit similar to a smoke alarm which should be included in every home, especially those with gas equipment and fireplaces or furnaces.

Faulty septic systems. Inspections of septic systems are important because these systems take wastewater from the property, remove most of the contaminants, and then put the water into the soil. If the system is faulty, it can be releasing contaminated water into the soil, thereby contaminating the soil. Potential buyers and septic system users should have the county health department conduct an inspection of the system.

Illegal drug manufacturing. Manufacturing illegal drugs such as methamphetamine produces highly toxic fumes that last a long time. Continued exposure to the fumes can cause fatal burns to the lungs, can damage the liver and spleen, and can lead to learning disabilities. Any property suspected as having been a place for drug manufacturing should be investigated prior to being sold or leased, and the possible health hazards must be disclosed to the potential buyer or renter.

Radon. This is the easiest hazard to detect and mitigate. It is an odorless, colorless, tasteless, and radioactive gas that is created in the ground where uranium and radium exist. Prolonged exposure to radon can cause lung cancer. It can enter the home through any cracks, gaps, or cavities, including crawl spaces and openings around pipes. It can be easily detected by a radon test, so home inspections should include this test.

Urea formaldehyde. This type of hazard is found in foam thermal insulation in homes built before 1980. The formaldehyde gas emissions from the insulation decrease over time, so most homes with the insulation no longer pose a threat. The most common sources of formaldehyde in a home are pressed wood products such as particleboard, hardwood plywood paneling, and medium density fiberboard. Plastic furniture, new carpeting, and other vinyl materials also emit formaldehyde gases during the first few months after installation. Formaldehyde can cause eye problems, nausea, breathing problems, and allergic reactions.

Leaking underground storage tanks. USTs have at least 10 percent of their volume underground and are used to store fuel oil, gasoline, and other toxic fluids. Tanks made of steel can corrode over time and leak their contents into the surrounding soil, contaminating groundwater. They also provide a potential for fire and explosion. Tank removal is expensive, so removal is not common. Therefore, potential buyers must be informed of the presence of a UST on the property and of the health and financial risks of purchasing a property that contains a UST.

Environmental legislation

Clean Air and Clean Water Acts. The Clean Air Act of 1963, since amended a number of times, was designed to control air pollution on a national level. Among other things, the act authorizes the setting of standards for controlling the emission of pollutants and monitoring air quality. It identifies hazardous air pollutants such as formaldehyde and regulates their use. Importantly, the act allows private citizens to sue other citizens to enforce the law.

The Clean Water Act, officially known as the Federal Water Pollution Control Act Amendments of 1972, together with revisions contained in the Clean Water Act of 1977 and the Water Quality Act of 1987, is the primary federal law governing water pollution. It applies to all waters connected with navigable waters, but the interpretation of exactly which waters are covered remains open to dispute. The Clean Water Act does not directly deal with groundwater contamination, which is addressed in the Safe Drinking Water Act, Resource Conservation and Recovery Act, and the Superfund act.

Safe Drinking Water Act. Congress passed the Safe Drinking Water Act (SDWA) in 1974 (amended 1986 and 1996) to regulate and protect the public supply of drinking water. The act authorizes the setting of standards, protection of water sources, training of operators, funding of improvements, and dissemination of information. Under the act, water suppliers must report health risks to the EPA within 24 hours of discovery. Hydraulic fracturing (fracking) oil and gas production poses one of the greatest current threats to groundwater.

Property sellers generally must disclose the source of drinking water for the property and the presence, type and location of any septic system on the property. A water supply other than a municipal one and any septic system other than a standard one should be tested.

Brownfields Law. Brownfields are abandoned commercial or industrial sites that are likely to contain toxic material. The Small Business Liability Relief and Brownfields Revitalization Act (known as the Brownfields Law), passed in 2002 provides clean-up funds, liability protections, and tax incentives to reclaim contaminated properties. Under this law, owners who neither caused nor contributed to the contamination are released from liability for the clean up.

Environmental Protection Agency. The EPA was established on December 2, 1970 to bring together federal research, monitoring, standard-setting and enforcement activities into one agency dedicated to environmental protection. The EPA, working with state, local, and tribal governments, enforces the Clean Air and Clean Water Acts along with other environmental laws.

Disclosure obligations and liabilities

As discussed in an earlier chapter, licensees are expected to be aware of environmental issues and to know where to look for professional help. They are not expected to have expert knowledge of environmental law nor of physical conditions in a property. Rather, they must treat potential environmental hazards in the same way that they treat other material facts about a property: disclosure. It is advisable to have an attorney draft the appropriate disclosures to lessen the broker's liability should problems occur in the future. In sum, for their own protection, licensees should be careful to:

- recognize potential hazards
- disclose known material facts
- distribute the HUD booklet
- know where to seek professional help.

INSPECTIONS

Process

Property inspections may identify builder oversights or the need for major repairs. They may also identify the need for regular maintenance to keep the property in good condition. In addition to looking for structural issues, plumbing and electrical problems, and roof and foundation issues, inspections can uncover termites or other pests that are damaging the structure. Inspections can also uncover environmental issues that have a detrimental impact on the property.

Environmental inspections

Home inspections should include looking for common environmental issues that can affect the property and the residents of the property. Environmental hazards can have a significant impact on the sale of a property. An environmental site assessment (ESA) may be conducted to identify environmental impairments and protect parties against becoming involved in contamination issues. Such assessments are performed in three phases. A Phase 1 ESA identifies potential problems on or near the subject property. A Phase 2 ESA involves active testing of soil, water, and other components of the subject property.

Agent disclosure duties

Most states require disclosure of known material facts regarding residential properties of one to four units. If a licensee knows the result of an inspection, this is a material fact to be disclosed. Disclosure of environmental issues on commercial and industrial properties is often not mandated. Where disclosure is not required, real estate licensees should suggest the use of a professional environmental audit.

SOUTH CAROLINA RESIDENTIAL PROPERTY CONDITION DISCLOSURE

Affected transactions

South Carolina law requires sellers to disclose any known material defects to potential buyers using a special property condition disclosure form for this purpose. For a residential property of at least one but not more than four units, disclosing the property's condition is required with the following transactions:

- the sale or exchange of property
- an installment land sales contract
- a lease with an option to purchase

Disclosure exceptions. South Carolina law does not require disclosures for the following property transfers:

- ordered by a court including
  - in the administration of an estate
  - by a writ of execution
  - by foreclosure sale
  - by a trustee in bankruptcy
  - transfers by eminent domain
  - from a decree of specific performance
- by a mortgagee who acquired the property through a foreclosure
- by a fiduciary in the course of the administration of a decedent's estate, guardianship, conservatorship, or trust
- from one or more co-owners solely to one or more other co-owners
- made solely to a spouse or a blood relative of one or more transferors
- between spouses resulting from a divorce decree, support order, or marital property distribution order
- made because of the record owner's failure to pay federal, state, or local taxes
- to or from the federal government
- to the State, its agencies and departments, and its political subdivisions including school districts
- involving the first sale of a dwelling never inhabited
- real property sold at public auction
- to a residential trust
- a vacation time sharing plan as defined in SC law
- a vacation multiple ownership interest
- between parties when both parties agree in writing not to complete a disclosure statement

Contents of the property condition disclosure form

When a property condition disclosure is required, the owner must provide to a purchaser a written disclosure statement that contains the language and be in the form promulgated by the Commission. The Commission may charge a reasonable fee for the printed form but it will also post the form for free downloading on its public website. The mandatory form (effective 1-1-2019) can be downloaded at:

https://llr.sc.gov/re/recpdf/Property-Condition-Disclosure-Statement-06.01.2023.pdf

South Carolina law requires that the disclosure statement include information about the following:

- water supply and sanitary sewage disposal system
- roof, chimneys, floors, foundation, basement, and other structural components and modifications of these structural components
- plumbing, electrical, heating, cooling, and other mechanical systems
- current or prior infestations of wood-destroying insects or organisms
- whether any zoning laws, building codes, boundary disputes, or easements affect the property
- the presence of lead-based paint, asbestos, radon gas, methane gas, or toxic material
- whether there are any operable rental or lease agreements on the property and, if known, any outstanding charges the tenant owes for gas, electric, water, sewage, or garbage services
- existence of a meter conservation charge that applies to electricity or natural gas service to the property
- any designations as a historic building, landmark, site, or other historic district that may limit changes, renovations or demolitions (Sec. V, #16)
- whether the property is subject to a homeowners association's governance which imposes usage restrictions and financial obligations; if HOA is present, seller must complete SC RPCDS Addendum (Sec IX)

The disclosure statement must allow the owner to indicate that the owner has actual knowledge of the conditions or is making no representation as to condition. According to the statute a seller may deliver the disclosure to the buyer electronically through the Internet or other similar methods.

Further considerations

The listing agent is responsible for informing the seller in writing of the seller's obligation to provide a property disclosure. Putting this in writing to the seller relieves the listing agent of any liability for the seller's refusal or failure to provide the property disclosure to a buyer.

Delivery. A seller who is required to deliver a property disclosure must do so before the seller and buyer sign a real estate contract, unless the contract states otherwise.

Failure to provide the disclosure to the buyer does not

- void the agreement
- create a defect in the title
- present a valid reason to delay or interfere with the closing of the transaction

Corrected disclosure statements. If after delivery a seller discovers an inaccuracy in the statement or the disclosure becomes inaccurate because some event occurs, the seller must deliver a corrected disclosure statement to the buyer or make repairs necessitated by the event before closing.

False disclosure. A seller who knowingly discloses false, incomplete, or misleading information on the disclosure statement is liable for actual damages to the buyer, as well as court costs and reasonable attorney fees. Neither the listing agent nor the selling agent is liable to a buyer if

- the seller gives the buyer a disclosure that has false, incomplete, or misleading information and

- the licensee did not know or have reason to suspect the information was false, incomplete, or misleading

Buyer inspection. The seller's providing of a property condition disclosure does not affect the buyer's obligation to inspect the property and its improvements. Neither the listing agent nor the selling agent has any duty to inspect the onsite or offsite conditions of the property.

Psychologically affected property. A seller is not required to disclose on the property condition statement the fact or suspicion that the property is psychologically affected or "stigmatized."

SNAPSHOT REVIEW:

Unit 2: PROPERTY DISCLOSURE

PROPERTY CONDITION AND MATERIAL FACTS
Duty to inform

- agent must inform client of all material facts, reports, rumors affecting client's interests in property transaction
- disclosure areas: property condition, title defects, environmental hazards, property defects

Red flag issues

- agent who sees "red flag" issue should advise seller to seek expert advice
- includes environmental concerns; property anomalies; neighborhood issues; poor construction; signs of flooding; poor floorplan; adjacent property features

ENVIRONMENTAL HAZARDS
Specific environmental hazards and issues

- **Lead-based paint.** Found in most homes built before 1978
- **Mold.** Fungus grows under moist conditions and can cause allergic reactions
- **Asbestos.** Can cause lung cancer if dust filters into air
- **Air quality.** Can be affected by numerous things
- **Water quality.** Ground water easily contaminated; EPA sets standards for protecting ground water
- **Carbon monoxide.** Odorless, colorless, toxic gas
- **Faulty septic systems.** Faulty systems can release contaminated wastewater into soil
- **Illegal drug manufacturing.** Methamphetamine produces highly toxic fumes
- **Radon.** Odorless, colorless, tasteless, radioactive gas created in ground where uranium and radium exist; exposure can cause cancer
- **Urea formaldehyde.** Found in foam thermal insulation in homes built before 1980
- **Leaking underground storage tanks.** USTs have 10% of volume underground and store fuel oil, gasoline, and other toxic fluids. Can contaminate soil and groundwater

Environmental legislation

- **The Clean Air Act of 1963.** Controls air pollution on national level; standards controlling emission of pollutants and monitoring air quality
- **Clean Water Act (or Federal Water Pollution Control Act Amendments of 1972).** Governs water pollution of all waters connected by navigable waters. Does not directly deal with groundwater contamination
- **Safe Drinking Water Act.** Regulates and protects public supply of drinking water
- **Brownfields Law.** Clean-up funds, liability protections and tax incentives to reclaim contaminated properties
- **Environmental Protection Agency.** Combines federal research, monitoring, standard-setting, enforcement activities into one agency dedicated to environmental protection

Disclosure obligations and liabilities

- licensees should recognize potential hazards; disclose known material facts; distribute the HUD booklet; know where to seek professional help

INSPECTIONS
Process

- identify builder oversights, need for major repairs, or need for regular maintenance
- includes structural components, plumbing, electrical, roof, foundation, termite, and pest inspections

Environmental inspections

- environmental site assessment to identify environmental impairments
- Phase 1 ESA identifies potential problems; Phase 2 ESA involves active testing of soil, water, and other components

Agent disclosure duties

- disclosure of known material facts regarding residential properties of one- to four- units are required

SOUTH CAROLINA RESIDENTIAL PROPERTY CONDITION DISCLOSURE
Affected transactions

- sellers disclose known material defects to potential buyers using special property condition disclosure form
- property condition disclosures required for sale or exchange of property; installment land sales contract; lease with option to purchase
- disclosures not required for
  - property transfers ordered by a court;
  - mortgagee who acquired property through foreclosure;
  - by fiduciary in course of administration of decedent's estate;
  - guardianship, conservatorship, trust;
  - from one or more co-owners solely to one or more other co-owners;
  - made solely to a spouse or a blood relative of one or more transferors;
  - between spouses resulting from a divorce decree, support order, or marital property distribution order;
  - made because of the record owner's failure to pay federal, state, or local taxes;
  - to or from the federal government; to the State;
  - involving the first sale of a dwelling never inhabited;
  - real property sold at public auction;
  - to a residential trust;
  - a vacation time sharing plan as defined in SC law;
  - a vacation multiple ownership interest;
  - between parties when both parties agree in writing not to complete a disclosure statement

Contents of the form

- must include information about:
  - water supply and sanitary sewage disposal system;

- o roof, chimneys, floors, foundation, basement,
- o plumbing, electrical, heating, cooling, and other mechanical systems;
- o current or prior infestations of wood-destroying insects or organisms, etc.
- must allow owner to indicate that owner has actual knowledge of conditions or is making no representation as to condition

Further considerations

- listing agent inform seller in writing of seller's obligation to provide property disclosure
- **Delivery.** seller must deliver property disclosure before real estate contract signed
- **Corrected disclosure statements.** seller must deliver a corrected disclosure statement to buyer or make repairs before closing.
- **False disclosure.** Seller who knowingly discloses false, incomplete, or misleading information on disclosure statement liable for actual damages to buyer, court costs, reasonable attorney fees
- **Buyer inspection.** seller's providing of property condition disclosure does not affect buyer's obligation to inspect property and its improvements.
- **Psychologically affected property.** Seller not required to disclose on property condition statement that property is psychologically affected or "stigmatized"

Check Your Understanding Quiz:

Unit 2: Property Disclosure

Carefully read each question and provide your best answer based on what you learned in this module. Then check your answers against the Answer Key which immediately follows the quiz questions.

1. Which type of environmental hazard is found in foam thermal insulation?

    a. Urea formaldehyde
    b. Radon
    c. UST
    d. Lead

2. Which statute governs water pollution in all navigable waters?

    a. Clean Air Act of 1963
    b. Water Quality Act of 1987
    c. Safe Drinking Water Act
    d. Environmental Protections Act

3. What are abandoned commercial sites that contain toxic materials called?

    a. USTs
    b. Landfills
    c. Brownfields
    d. Wastelands

4. Which of the following transactions does not require property disclosures?

    a. Quadplex
    b. Foreclosure sale
    c. An installment land sales contract
    d. A lease with option to buy

5. Which of the following hazards is odorless, colorless, tasteless and radioactive?

    a. Gasoline
    b. Urea formaldehyde
    c. Underground septic tank
    d. Radon

6. Which of the following is not a material fact required to be disclosed?

    a. Murder that occurred on the property
    b. Title defect
    c. Agent's opinion of property condition
    d. Environmental hazard

7. Which of the following is a fungus that grows under moist conditions?

    a. Asbestos
    b. Mold
    c. Lead
    d. Urea

8. Which agency brings together federal research, monitoring, and enforcement activities into one agency dedicated to environmental protection?

    a. Brownfields Agency
    b. WHO
    c. EPA
    d. Earth Agency

9. In order to identify environmental impairments, a(n) _____ may be conducted.

    a. environmental site assessment
    b. property site inspection
    c. EPA appraisal
    d. geological assessment

10. A leaking chimney can release _____.

    a. radon.
    b. carbon monoxide.
    c. mold.
    d. sulfur.

Exercise Workshop -- Unit 2: Property Disclosure

Exercise 2-1. Property Disclosure

Synopsis:

In this exercise, you will identify items discovered while helping a seller complete a Property Disclosure Form.

Instructions:

1. Read the following passage.
2. Identify items that must be disclosed on the Property Disclosure Form.

Activity:

Agent Ron is helping his seller complete the Property Disclosure Form. Ron has asked the sellers to walk him around their home and point out any items that will need to be disclosed to potential buyers.

The house was built in 1974 and is a two-bedroom, two-bath home with a total of 2,000 square feet. The house was constructed with concrete block. The walls are insulated and finished with drywall.

While going through the home with the seller, Agent Ron noticed a water stain in the guest bathroom ceiling. When he inquired about the stain, he was told there had been a leak in the roof, but they had fixed it but never fixed the bathroom ceiling.

Agent Ron also noticed that the basement was not ventilated to the outside and showed signs of mildew around the ceiling vent.

Agent Ron asked if the home was on city water and was informed that there was a septic tank and well on the property.

The seller also informs Ron that the house is haunted because of a double homicide that occurred there ten years ago. They also told Ron that there was a sex offender who lived around the block.

What should Ron ensure is included in disclosures for this piece of property?

Unit 3: Other Brokerage Disclosures

Unit 3: Other brokerage disclosures – Learning Objectives

When the student has completed Unit 3, he or she will be able to:

1. Characterize the licensee's disclosure duties with respect to selling one's own property; selling stigmatized property; selling property as-is; and Megan's Law

---

TRANSACTING LICENSEE'S OWN PROPERTY

Section 40-57-135(F) of the license law states that

- a licensee must clearly reveal the license status in a personal real estate transaction.

The licensee must reveal this status at first substantive contact with a consumer and in advertising or marketing in any media. A licensee must disclose this licensed status in bold, underlined capital letters on the first page of the contract for the purchase, sale, exchange, rental, or lease of real property.

- the licensee must deposit monies received in a personal rental or real estate transaction in the licensee's personal trust account.

These funds may not be deposited in the real estate brokerage firm's trust account unless the real estate brokerage firm manages, lists, or owns the real property.

If a licensee wishes to purchase real estate listed with the affiliated brokerage firm, the broker-in-charge must ensure that the licensee first makes the status as a licensee clearly known in writing to all parties involved. Upon request of the commission, the broker-in-charge will provide evidence of the licensee having made this disclosure, including any of the following:

- purchases made directly or indirectly by the licensee
- purchases made for the licensee's own account or for a corporation or another business in which the licensee holds an interest
- purchases made for a close relative
- real estate for which the licensee has been approached by the seller or prospective buyer to act as agent

in order for a real estate brokerage firm to claim a fee for the sale of a listed property to a supervised licensee, a separate written agreement signed by the seller client must acknowledge the purchaser as a licensee affiliated with the firm and recognize the right of the seller not to pay the brokerage fee.

STIGMATIZED PROPERTY

Stigmatized property is property which buyers or tenants may reject for reasons that are unrelated to its physical condition or features. According to the license law, an owner of real estate or licensed real estate agent of any party to a transaction cannot be sued for failure to disclose in a transaction

- that the subject property is or was occupied by an individual who was infected with a virus or any other disease, such as HIV, which has been determined by medical evidence as being highly unlikely to be transmitted through occupancy of a dwelling
- that an occupant of a property died there or the manner of the death
- any off-site condition or hazard that does not directly impact the property being transferred
- any psychological impact that has no material impact on the physical condition of the property being transferred

A buyer or prospective buyer may still bring an action against an owner of real estate or the agent of an owner who makes intentional misrepresentations in response to a direct inquiry with regard to psychological impacts, offsite conditions, or stigmas associated with the real estate.

"AS-IS" PROPERTY

The requirement for certain property disclosures does not prevent parties from entering into agreements with respect to the physical condition of the property, including an agreement to sell the property "as is." In other words, despite the presence of certain disclosure obligations, principal parties may legally sell real properties on an "as-is" basis.

MEGAN'S LAW

Salient provisions
Megan's Law is the name for a federal law, and informal name for subsequent state laws, in the United States requiring law enforcement authorities to make information available to the public regarding registered sex offenders. The laws were created in response to the murder of Megan Kanka.

Individual states decide what information will be made available and how it should be disseminated. Commonly included information is the offender's name, picture, address, incarceration date, and offense of conviction. The information is often displayed on free public websites, but can be published in newspapers, distributed in pamphlets, or through various other means.

Sex offender registry (SORT). South Carolina uses a sex offender management application called SORT. SORT is provided at no charge by the U.S. Department of Justice to the State of South Carolina. SORT is designed to make the sex offender registry process as efficient and effective as possible. This streamlined process also provides improved information sharing across all jurisdictions. SORT provides community notifications and automatic updates to the National Sex Offender Public Web Site. Other features include multiple photographs of the offender over time, a visual map of where the offender lives, a list of aliases the offender has used in the past, and a list of all of the sexually related offenses that an offender has been convicted of committing.

Disclosure

Real estate licensees do not have an affirmative duty under Megan's Law to investigate and disclose the presence of registered offenders. However, licensees should be mindful that this does not serve to release them of all responsibility. For a buyer agent to conform to the standards of practice applicable to selling residential real estate, the buyer agent should at least be advising the buyers of their ability to determine the presence of registered offenders in adjacent and nearby properties.

SNAPSHOT REVIEW:

Unit 3: OTHER BROKERAGE DISCLOSURES

TRANSACTING LICENSEE'S OWN PROPERTY

- licensees must reveal license status in personal real estate transactions

STIGMATIZED PROPERTY

- property buyers or tenants may refuse to purchase a property for reasons unrelated to its physical condition or features
- disclosures not required if subject property is/was
    - occupied by individual infected with virus
    - an occupant died on premises
    - there is an off-site condition or hazard that does not directly impact property being transferred
    - where there may be a psychological impact that has no material impact on property

"AS-IS" PROPERTY

- requirement for property disclosures does not prevent parties from entering agreements, including selling property "as is"

MEGAN'S LAW

- requires law enforcement authorities make information available to public regarding registered sex offenders

Salient provisions

- individual states decide what information made available
- SORT is a sex offender management application used in SC
- SORT streamlines the sex offender registry process and updates National Sex Offender Public Web Site

Disclosure

- licensees do not have to investigate and disclose presence of registered offenders
- buyer agent should advise buyers of their ability to determine presence of registered offenders

===

Check Your Understanding Quiz:

Unit 3: Other Brokerage Disclosures

Carefully read each question and provide your best answer based on what you learned in this module. Then check your answers against the Answer Key which immediately follows the quiz questions.

1. Which statute requires law enforcement to make public any information about registered sex offenders?

    a. Megan's Law
    b. Angela's Law
    c. Public Disclosure Law
    d. Criminal Acts Law

2. What is the term or phrase describing a property where buyers refuse to buy for reasons unrelated to physical condition?

    a. Defected property
    b. Taboo property
    c. Stigmatized property
    d. Untransferable property

3. Andrew refuses to do any repairs and wants to sell his property in its current state. What condition is he selling the home in?

    a. Defected condition
    b. As-Is condition
    c. Uninhabitable condition
    d. Foreclosed condition

4. Where in the sale contract must a licensee disclose his or her licensee status on personal transactions?

    a. On the last page of the contract
    b. On an addendum attached to the contract
    c. On the first page of the contract
    d. The licensee does not need to disclose his or her licensee status in writing.

5. What is South Carolina's sex offender management application called?

    a. OFF
    b. SEA
    c. SORT
    d. NSOP

6. Who pays for the sex offender management application?

    a. OFF
    b. SEA
    c. SORT
    d. It is provided at no charge by the U.S. Department of Justice to the State of South Carolina.

7. What is a buyer's agent required to do with respect to informing buyers about local sex offenders?

    a. Buyer's agents must advise buyers of their ability to determine the presence of registered offenders.
    b. Buyer's agents must research if there are any sex offenders present and inform their clients.
    c. Buyer's agents cannot mention anything regarding sex offenders.
    d. Buyer's agents are not required to mention anything regarding sex offenders.

8. Chase is a real estate agent and wants to buy his first house. What must he tell the listing agent?

    a. Chase does not need to disclose anything to the listing agent.
    b. Chase does not need to tell the listing agent until closing day.
    c. Chase only needs to tell the sellers if he sees them in person.
    d. Chase must disclose his license status to all parties involved.

9. Which of the following constitutes a stigmatized property

    a. Subject property has lead paint
    b. Property has asbestos
    c. Subject property is occupied by an individual infected with HIV
    d. Property has signs of mold

10. Who decides what information regarding sex offenders is made public?

    a. Individual states
    b. Local counties
    c. Real estate board
    d. Federal government

Module B: REAL ESTATE CONTRACTS

Unit 4: Essential Contract Law Review

Unit 5: Listing Agreements

Unit 6: Purchase and Sale Contracts

Unit 7: Option-to-Buy Contracts

Unit 8: Contracts for Deed

Module B Learning Objectives

Essential Contract Law Review

> 1. Summarize the essential cornerstones of contract validity, contract creation, and how contracts are terminated

Listing Agreements

> 1. Summarize the salient types of South Carolina listings, required clauses, and how licensees ultimately earn compensation

Purchase and Sale Contracts

> 1. Characterize the central provisions of South Carolina purchase and sale contracts and the licensee's role in completing such agreements

> 2. Describe how licensees can properly avoid the unauthorized practice of law with respect to contract completion

Option-to-Buy Contracts

> 1. Describe the essential requirements of a valid option-to-purchase contract and its central provisions

Contracts for Deed

> 1. Describe the salient mechanics of a contract for deed and how this transaction differs from conventional conveyances with respect to enforcement and legal title

Unit 4: Essential Contract Law Review

When the student has completed Unit 4, he or she will be able to:

> **1. Summarize the essential cornerstones of contract validity, contract creation, and how contracts are terminated**

CONTRACT VALIDITY AND ENFORCEABILITY

Real estate contracts are the legal agreements that underlie the transfer and financing of real estate, as well as the real estate brokerage business. Sale and lease contracts and option agreements are used to transfer real estate interests from one party to another. Mortgage contracts and promissory agreements are part of financing real estate. Listing and representation contracts establish client relationships and provide for compensation.

In order to work with real estate contracts, it is imperative first to grasp basic concepts that apply to all contracts in general. These concepts provide a foundation for understanding the specifics of particular types of real estate contract.

A contract is an agreement between two or more parties who, in a "meeting of the minds," have pledged to perform or refrain from performing some act. A valid contract is one that is legally enforceable by virtue of meeting certain requirements of contract law.

If a contract does not meet the requirements, it is not valid and the parties to it cannot resort to a court of law to enforce its provisions.

Note that a contract is not a legal form or a prescribed set of words in a document, but rather the intangible agreement that was made in "the meeting of the minds" of the parties to the contract.

Contract validity requirements

The essential variables that determine a contracts validity are:

- competent parties
- mutual consent
- valuable consideration
- legal purpose
- voluntary act of good faith

Competent parties. The parties to a contract must have the capacity to contract, and there must be at least two such parties. Thus, the owner of a tenancy for life cannot deed his interest to himself in the form of a fee simple, as this would involve only one party. Capacity to contract is determined by three factors:

- legal age
- mental competency
- legitimate authority

To be mentally competent, a party must have sufficient understanding of the import and consequences of a contract. Competency in this context is separate and distinct from sanity. Incompetent parties, or parties of "unsound mind," may not enter into enforceable contracts. The incompetency of a party may be ruled by a court of law or by other means. In some areas, convicted felons may be deemed incompetent, depending on the nature of the crime.

Mutual consent. Mutual consent, also known as offer and acceptance and meeting of the minds, requires that a contract involve a clear and definite offer and an intentional, unqualified acceptance of the offer. In effect, the parties must agree to the terms without equivocation. A court may nullify a contract where the acceptance of terms by either party was partial, accidental, or vague.

Valuable consideration. A contract must contain a two-way exchange of valuable consideration as compensation for performance by the other party. The exchange of considerations must be two-way. The contract is not valid or enforceable if just one party provides consideration.

Valuable consideration can be something of tangible value, such as money or something a party promises to do or not do. For example, a home builder may promise to build a house for a party as consideration for receiving money from the home buyer. Or, a landowner may agree not to sell a property as consideration for a developer's option money. Also, valuable consideration can be something intangible that a party must give up, such as a homeowner's occupancy of the house in exchange for rent. In effect, consideration is the price one party must pay to obtain performance from the other party.

Legal purpose. The content, promise, or intent of a contract must be lawful. A contract that proposes an illegal act is void.

Voluntary, good faith act. The parties must create the contract in good faith as a free and voluntary act. A contract is thus voidable if one party acted under duress, coercion, fraud, or misrepresentation. For example, if a property seller induces a buyer to purchase a house based on assurances that the roof is new, the buyer may rescind the agreement if the roof turns out to be twenty years old and leaky.

Conveyance contracts. In addition to satisfying the foregoing requirements, a contract that conveys an interest in real estate must:

- be in writing
- contain a legal description of the property
- be signed by one or more of the parties

A lease contract that has a term of one year or less is an exception. Such leases do not have to be in writing to be enforceable.

Enforcement limitations

Certain contracts that fail to meet the validity requirements are voidable if a damaged party takes appropriate action. The enforcement of voidable contracts, however, is limited by statutes of limitation. Certain other contracts which are valid may not be enforceable due to the statute of frauds.

Statute of limitations. The statute of limitations restricts the time period for which an injured party in a contract has the right to rescind or disaffirm the contract. A party to a voidable contract must act within the statutory period.

Statute of frauds. The statute of frauds requires that certain contracts must be in writing to be enforceable. Real estate contracts that convey an interest in real property fall in this category, with the exception that a lease of one year's duration or less may be oral. All other contracts to buy, sell, exchange, or lease interests in real property must be in writing to be enforceable. In addition, listing agreements in most states must be in writing.

The statute of frauds concerns the enforceability of a contract, not its validity. Once the parties to a valid oral contract have executed and performed it, even if the contract was unenforceable, a party cannot use the Statute of Frauds to rescind the contract.

For example, a broker and a seller have an oral listing agreement. Following the terms of the agreement, the broker finds a buyer, and the seller pays the commission. They have now executed the contract, and the seller cannot later force the broker to return the commission based on the statute of frauds.

Uniform Electronic Transactions Act

Contracting electronically through email and fax greatly facilitates the completion of transactions. Clients, lenders, title agents, inspectors, brokers, and other participants in a transaction can quickly share documentation and information. Electronic contracting is made possible by the Uniform Electronic Transactions Act (UETA) and the Electronic Signatures in Global and National Commerce Act (E-Sign), which are federal laws. UETA, which has been accepted in most states, provides that electronic records and signatures are legal and must be accepted. E-Sign makes contracts, records, and signatures legally enforceable, regardless of medium, even where UETA is not accepted.

CONTRACT CREATION

Offer and acceptance

The mutual consent required for a valid contract is reached through the process of offer and acceptance: The offeror proposes contract terms in an offer to the offeree. If the offeree accepts all terms without amendment, the offer becomes a contract. The exact point at which the offer becomes a contract is when the offeree gives the offeror notice of the acceptance.

Offer, Counteroffer and Acceptance

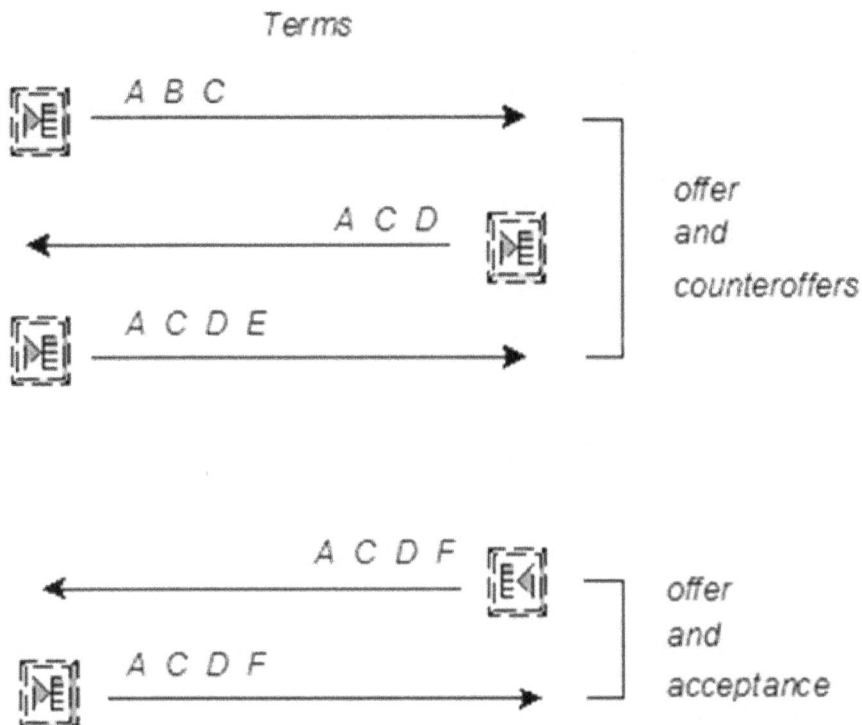

Terms

A B C → offer and counteroffers

A C D ←

A C D E →

A C D F ← offer and acceptance

A C D F →

Offer. An offer expresses the offeror's intention to enter into a contract with an offeree to perform the terms of the agreement in exchange for the offeree's performance. In a real estate sale or lease contract, the offer must clearly contain all intended terms of the contract in writing and be communicated to the offeree.

If an offer contains an expiration date and the phrase "time is of the essence," the offer expires at exactly the time specified. In the absence of a stated time period, the offeree has a "reasonable" time to accept an offer.

Acceptance. An offer gives the offeree the power of accepting. For an acceptance to be valid, the offeree must manifestly and unequivocally accept all terms of the offer without change, and so indicate by signing the offer, preferably with a date of signing. The acceptance must then be communicated to the offeror. If the communication of acceptance is by mail, the offer is considered to be communicated as soon as it is placed in the mail.

Counteroffer. By changing any of the terms of an offer, the offeree creates a counteroffer, and the original offer is void. At this point, the offeree becomes the offeror, and the new offeree gains the right of acceptance. If accepted, the counteroffer becomes a valid contract provided all other requirements are met.

For example, a seller changes the expiration date of a buyer's offer by one day, signs the offer and returns it to the buyer. The single amendment extinguishes the buyer's offer, and the buyer is no longer bound by any agreement. The seller's amended offer is a counteroffer which now gives the buyer the right of acceptance. If the buyer accepts the counteroffer, the counteroffer becomes a binding contract

Offer termination. Any of the following actions or circumstances can terminate an offer:

- acceptance: the offeree accepts the offer, converting it to a contract
- rejection: the offeree rejects the offer
- revocation: the offeror withdraws the offer before acceptance
- lapse of time: the offer expires
- counteroffer: the offeree changes the offer
- death or insanity of either party

CONTRACT TERMINATION

Termination of a contract, also called cancellation and discharge, may occur for any of the following causes: performance; infeasibility; mutual agreement; rescission; revocation; abandonment; lapse of time; or invalidity.

Forms of contract termination

Performance. A contract terminates when fully performed by the parties. It may also terminate for:

- partial performance, if the parties agree
- sufficient performance, if a court determines a party has sufficiently performed the contract, even though not to the full extent of every provision

Infeasibility. An otherwise valid contract can be canceled if it is not possible to perform. Certain personal services contracts, for example, depend on the unique capabilities of one person which cannot be substituted by someone else. If such a person dies or is sufficiently disabled, the contract is cancelable.

Mutual agreement. Parties to a contract can agree to terminate, or renounce, the contract. If the parties wish to create a new contract to replace the cancelled contract, they must comply with the validity requirements for the new contract. Such substitution is called novation.

Cooling-period rescission. Rescission is the act of nullifying a contract where parties to certain contracts are allowed a statutory amount of time after entering into a contract, or "cooling period", to rescind the contract without cause. No reason need be stated for the cancellation, and the cancelling party incurs no liability for performance.

For example, consider the unsuspecting buyer of a lot in a new resort development. Such buyers are often the targets of hard-sell tactics which lead to a completed sales contract and a deposit. The statutory cooling period gives the buyer an opportunity to reconsider the investment in the absence of the persistent salesperson.

Revocation. Revocation is cancellation of the contract by one party without the consent of the other. For example, a seller may revoke a listing to take the property off the market. While all parties have the power to revoke, they may not have a defensible right. In the absence of justifiable grounds, a revocation may not relieve the revoking party of contract obligations.

Abandonment. Abandonment occurs when parties fail to perform contract obligations. This situation may allow the parties to cancel the contract.

Lapse of time. If a contract contains an expiration provision and date, the contract automatically expires on the deadline.

Invalidity of contract. If a contract is void, it terminates without the need for disaffirmation. A voidable contract can be cancelled by operation of law or by rescission.

Breach of contract and remedies

A breach of contract is a failure to perform according to the terms of the agreement. Also called default, a breach of contract gives the damaged party the right to take legal action.

The damaged party may elect the following legal remedies:

- rescission
- forfeiture
- suit for damages
- suit for specific performance

Rescission. A damaged party may rescind the contract. This cancels the contract and returns the parties to their pre-contract condition, including the refunding of any monies already transferred.

Forfeiture. A forfeiture requires the breaching party to give up something, according to the terms of the contract. For example, a buyer who defaults on a sales contract may have to forfeit the earnest money deposit.

Suit for damages. A damaged party may sue for money damages in civil court. The suit must be initiated within the time period allowed by the statute of limitations. When a contract states the total amount due to a damaged party in the event of a breach, the compensation is known as liquidated damages. If the contract does not specify the amount, the damaged party may sue in court for unliquidated damages.

Suit for specific performance. A suit for specific performance is an attempt to force the defaulting party to comply with the terms of the contract. Specific performance suits occur when it is difficult to identify damages because of the unique circumstances of the real property in question. The most common instance is a defaulted sale or lease contract where the buyer or seller wants the court to compel the defaulting party to go through with the transaction, even when the defaulter would prefer to pay a damage award.

SNAPSHOT REVIEW:

Unit 4: ESSENTIAL CONTRACT LAW REVIEW

CONTRACT VALIDITY AND ENFORCEABILITY

- contracts are legal agreements that underlie transfer and financing of real estate
- sale, lease, option agreements are used to transfer real estate interests from one party to another
- mortgage contracts and promissory agreements part of financing real estate
- listing and representation contracts establish client relationships and compensation

Contract validity requirements

- competent parties; mutual consent; valuable consideration; legal purpose; voluntary act of good faith
- **Competent parties**. Must be mentally competent, legal age, and have legitimate authority
- **Mutual consent.** Contract involve clear and definite offer and intentional, unqualified acceptance of offer
- **Valuable consideration.** Must contain two-way exchange of valuable consideration as compensation for performance by other party
- **Legal purpose.** Content, promise, or intent of contract must be lawful
- **Voluntary, good faith act.** Create contract in good faith as a free and voluntary act
- **Conveyance contracts.** Contract must be in writing; contain legal description of property; signed by one or more party

Enforcement limitations

- contracts voidable if damaged party takes appropriate action
- **Statute of limitations.** Restricts time period for which injured party has right to rescind or disaffirm contract
- **Statute of frauds.** Requires contracts be in writing to be enforceable

Uniform Electronic Transactions Act

- electronic records and signatures are legal and must be accepted

CONTRACT CREATION
Offer and acceptance

- **Offer.** Offeror's intention to enter contract with offeree to perform terms of agreement in exchange for offeree's performance
- **Acceptance.** Gives offeree power of accepting; if accepted, an enforceable contract is created
- **Counteroffer.** By changing terms of offer, offeree creates a counteroffer, and original offer is void
- **Offer termination.** Extinguished by acceptance; rejection; revocation; lapse of time; counteroffer; death or insanity

CONTRACT TERMINATION
Forms of contract termination

- **Performance.** Contract terminates when fully performed
- **Infeasibility.** Valid contract can be canceled if not possible to perform
- **Mutual agreement.** Parties to contract can agree to terminate or renounce contract
- **Cooling-period rescission.** Rescission is act of nullifying a contract where parties to certain contracts are allowed time after entering into contract, or "cooling period", to rescind contract without cause
- **Revocation.** Cancellation of contract by one party without consent of other
- **Abandonment.** When parties fail to perform contract obligations
- **Lapse of time.** If contract contains expiration provision and date, contract automatically expires on deadline
- **Invalidity of contract.** If contract is void, it terminates without need for disaffirmation

Breach of contract and remedies

- failure to perform according to terms of agreement
- called default
- gives damaged party right to take legal action
- **Rescission.** Damaged party may rescind contract
- **Forfeiture.** Requires breaching party to give up something
- **Suit for damages.** Damaged party may sue for money damages in civil court
- **Suit for specific performance.** Attempt to force defaulting party to comply with terms of contract

===

Check Your Understanding Quiz:

Unit 4: Essential Contract Law Review

Carefully read each question and provide your best answer based on what you learned in this module. Then check your answers against the Answer Key which immediately follows the quiz questions.

1. Electronic contracting is made possible by the _____.

   a. Uniform Electronic Transactions Act.
   b. Signature Act.
   c. Internet Transactions Act.
   d. Megan's Act.

2. Which form of contract termination allows a damaged party to cancel the contract?

   a. Forfeiture
   b. Specific performance
   c. Rescission
   d. Damaged suit

3. What is it called when one party cancels a contract without the consent of the other party?

   a. Misdemeanor
   b. Revocation
   c. Foreclosure
   d. Abandonment

4. The _____ allows a party to rescind a contract without cause.

   a. inspection period
   b. contingency period
   c. infeasibility period
   d. cooling period

5. By changing an offer term, the offeree creates a(n) _____ and the original offer is void.

   a. responsive offer
   b. accepted offer
   c. counteroffer
   d. bounced offer

6. What is it called if parties wish to substitute a new contract to replace the cancelled contract?

   a. Novation
   b. Revocation
   c. Placeholding
   d. This is not allowed.

7. If a contract is void, it _____.

   a. is abandoned.
   b. terminates without the need for disaffirmation.
   c. terminates only if a cancellation notice is signed.
   d. terminates within five days.

8. A buyer who defaults on a sales contract may _____.

   a. rescind the contract.
   b. be sued for infeasibility.
   c. get charged with abandonment.
   d. have to forfeit the earnest money deposit.

9. If a seller suddenly becomes disabled and is no longer able to perform, the contract is cancelable due to _____.

   a. infeasibility.
   b. specific performance.
   c. mutual agreement.
   d. revocation.

10. Which statute requires that contracts must be in writing to be enforceable?

   a. UETA
   b. The Validity Act
   c. The Statute of Frauds
   d. Verbal contracts are enforceable.

===

==

Exercise Workshop – Unit 4: Real Estate Contracts

Exercise 4-1. Contract Validity

Synopsis:

In this exercise, you will look at each situation and determine the validity of the contract. If it is not a valid contract, you should determine which required element(s) are missing.

Instructions:

1. Read each case carefully.
2. Decide if the situation describes a **valid contract**, **an unenforceable contract**, or a **voidable contract.**
3. If it is not a valid contract, identify why it is not a valid contract.
4. Check your answers against the answers below.

Exercise:

1. Sales Associate Mary leases an apartment to Robbie, a 17-year old college student. They agree upon the monthly rent, the length of the lease, and the payment date. Robbie signs the lease, and Mary sends it to the owner of the property to sign.

2. Buyer Allen submits an offer to buy Seller Jackie's house "as-Is" for $350,000 cash with closing in two weeks. Jackie agrees to Allen's price and terms. They sign the sales contract, and both uphold their end of the deal at closing.

3. John decides to sell his father's home and move his dad into a retirement community. He finds a buyer, and they agree upon a price and terms. Once the buyer and John sign the contract, John informs his dad of what he has done. His father does not want to sell his home, but John insists that they are under contract and must go through with the sale of the house.

4. Alex has a small farm where he grows cannabis. He enters into a contract to sell the farm to Walter. They agree upon the price, terms, and closing dating. They create a written sales contract which both of them sign.

5. Martha, the seller, and Max, the buyer, sign a contract to purchase Martha's vacation home. They have agreed upon the contract's price, terms, and dates, and both have freely signed the agreement. One part of the contract states that Max should have an escrow deposit delivered to Martha within five days of the contract signed by both parties. It is now seven days after the execution of the contract.

Exercise Workshop -- Unit 4: Real Estate Contracts

Exercise 4-2. Breaches & Remedies

Synopsis:

In this exercise, you will be the judge in a breach of contract case and decide what remedies should be given in the situation.

Instructions:

1. Read the case below carefully.
2. Identify key aspects of the case.
3. Decide how you would rule on this case.
4. Compare your decision to the actual verdict from the court

Activity:

Cindi and Tom looked at a condo in a new development. They spoke with the developer about changes they wished to see in the property. They agreed upon a price and Cindi, a real estate agent, created a Sales and Purchase Contract that both parties signed. Cindi and Tom gave the developer a $20,000 escrow deposit, and the developer agreed to do the upgrades Cindi and Tom had requested.

Cindi and Tom went to their bank to get a loan to pay for the property. They had a long history with the bank and saw nothing that would stop them from getting the loan. However, the bank returned that they qualified, but the bank would not be eligible for the condo complex.

Cindi and Tom went back to the developer stating they wanted to cancel the contract since they could not get financing. The developer told them that he could get financing for them. They told the developer that they did not want to go through with the contract if they could not get financing from their bank. They demanded the developer cancel the contract and give them back their escrow deposit.

Upon examination of the contract, it was noted that no financing contingency had been included in the contract. Also, the developer had made over $10,000 in an upgrade to the unit under contract.

The parties counter-sued each other. Cindi and Tom were requesting that the contract be rescinded and the developer filing suit for specific performance.

What would be your decision and remedy for this case?

Unit 5: Listing Agreements

Unit 5: Listing Agreements – Learning Objectives

When the student has completed Unit 5, he or she will be able to:

1. Summarize the salient types of South Carolina listings, required clauses, and how licensees ultimately earn compensation

TYPES OF LISTINGS

A broker may represent any principal party of a transaction: seller, landlord, buyer, tenant. An **owner listing** authorizes a broker to represent an owner or landlord. There are three main types of owner listing agreement: *exclusive right-to-sell* (or lease); *exclusive agency;* and *open listing*. Another type of listing, rarely used today, is a *net listing*. The first three forms differ in their statement of conditions under which the broker will be paid. The net listing is a variation on how much the broker will be paid

A **buyer agency** or **tenant representation agreement** authorizes a broker to represent a buyer or tenant. The most commonly used form is an *exclusive right-to-represent agreement*, the equivalent of an exclusive right-to-sell. However, exclusive agency and open types of agreement may be also used to secure a relationship on this side of a transaction.

Though not a distinct type of listing agreement, multiple listing is a significant feature of brokerage practice. Multiple listing is an authorization to enter a listing in a multiple listing service.

Types of Listing

Exclusive Right	$ ⇒ Broker	IF customer is procured
Exclusive Agency	$ ⇒ Broker	IF customer is procured and client does not procure
Open	$ ⇒ Broker	IF broker procures customer
Net	$ ⇒ Broker	IF customer is due commission, receives proceeds over seller's minimum
"Multiple Listing"	$ ⇒ Broker	Authority to enter listing in multiple listing service

Exclusive right-to-sell listing

The exclusive right-to-sell, also called exclusive authorization-to-sell and, simply, the exclusive, is the most widely used owner agreement. Under the terms of this listing, a seller contracts exclusively with a single broker to procure a buyer or effect a sale transaction. If a buyer is procured during the listing period, the broker is entitled to a commission, *regardless of who is procuring cause*. Thus, if anyone--the owner, another broker-- sells the property, the owner must pay the listing broker the contracted commission.

The exclusive right-to-lease is a similar contract for a leasing transaction. Under the terms of this listing, the owner or landlord must pay the listing broker a commission if anyone procures a tenant for the named premises. The exclusive listing gives the listing broker the greatest assurance of receiving compensation for marketing efforts.

Exclusive agency

An exclusive agency listing authorizes a single broker to sell the property and earn a commission, but leaves the owner the right to sell the property without the broker's assistance, in which case no commission is owed. Thus, if any party other than the owner is procuring cause in a completed sale of the property, including another broker, the contracted broker has earned the commission. This arrangement may also be used in a leasing transaction: if any party other than the owner procures the tenant, the owner must compensate the listing broker.

An exclusive agency listing generally must have an expiration date. Most states allow either an oral or written agreement.

Open listing

An open listing, or, simply, open, is a non-exclusive authorization to sell or lease a property. The owner may offer such agreements to any number of brokers in the marketplace. With an open listing, the broker who is the first to perform under the terms of the listing is the sole party entitled to a commission. Performance usually consists of being the procuring cause in the finding of a ready, willing, and able customer. If the transaction occurs without a procuring broker, no commissions are payable.

Open listings are rare in residential brokerage. Brokers generally shy away from them because they offer no assurance of compensation for marketing efforts. In addition, open listings cause commission disputes. To avoid such disputes, a broker has to register prospects with the owner to provide evidence of procuring cause in case a transaction results. An open listing may be oral or written.

Net listing

A net listing is one in which an owner sets a minimum acceptable amount to be received from the transaction and allows the broker to have any amount received in excess as a commission, assuming the broker has earned a commission according to the other terms of the agreement. The owner's "net" may or may not account for closing costs.

For example, a seller requires $750,000 for a property. A broker sells the property for $830,000 and receives the difference, $80,000, as commission.

Net listings are generally regarded as unprofessional today, and many states have outlawed them. The argument against the net listing is that it creates a conflict of interest for the broker. It is in the broker's interest to encourage the owner to put the lowest possible acceptable price in the listing, regardless of market value. Thus the agent violates fiduciary duty by failing to place the client's interests above those of the agent.

Buyer and tenant agency agreements

Buyer and tenant agency agreements create a fiduciary relationship with the buyer or tenant just as seller listings create a fiduciary relationship with the seller. Generally, buyer and tenant representation agreements are subject to the same laws and regulations as those applying to owner listings.

Duties of the agent. At the formation of the relationship, the buyer agent has the duty to explain how buyer or tenant agency relationships work. This is culminated by a signed agreement where the principal understands and accepts these circumstances. During the listing term, the buyer or tenant agent's principal duties are to diligently locate a property that meets the principal's requirements. In addition, the agent must comply with his or her state agency-disclosure laws which may differ from those of traditional listing agents. This involves timely disclosures to prospective sellers and their agents, usually upon initial contact

Transaction broker agreement

In terms of agency, a transaction broker is in a non-agency relationship with the seller or buyer. The agent is not bound by fiduciary duties to either party. Nevertheless, transaction brokers enter into binding agreements with buyers and sellers to complete transactions. Such agreements may be exclusive or non-exclusive. Like conventional listings, the transaction brokerage agreement binds the principal to a compensation agreement in the event the broker procures a property or a buyer. Typical agreements affirm the nature of the relationship, contain expiration dates, and describe the terms of the agreement, such as the type of property desired or the price a seller deems acceptable.

FULFILLMENT AND TERMINATION OF THE LISTING

A listing agreement may terminate in many ways. The only desirable and favorable way is by fulfillment of the contract. Fulfillment results when both parties have performed the actions they have promised to perform

Agent's performance

An agent performs a listing agreement by achieving the result specified in the agreement. When and if the result is achieved, the agent's performance is complete.

Find a customer or effect a transaction. A listing generally specifies the result to be either finding a customer or effecting a completed transaction.

Finding a customer means locating a party who is ready, willing, and able to transact under the client's terms. Effecting a completed transaction means finding a customer who is not only ready, willing, and able, but one who makes an acceptable offer.

A ready, willing, and able customer is one who is:

- amenable to the terms of the transaction (ready and willing)
- financially capable of paying the price and legally capable of completing the transaction (able)

Specific responsibilities. A listing agreement authorizes a broker to undertake actions relevant to achieving the performance objective. Authorized activities usually include the following:

- show or seek property
- locate buyer, seller, tenant, or landlord
- communicate the client's transaction terms
- promote features and advantages of the terms to customers
- assist in negotiating a meeting of the minds between parties

Due diligence. Due diligence in the listing context refers to verifying the accuracy of the statements in the listing regarding the property, the owner, and the owner's representations. Especially important facts for a broker or agent to verify are:

- the property condition
- ownership status
- the client's authority to act

Failure to perform a reasonable degree of due diligence may increase an agent's exposure to liability in the event that the property is not as represented or that the client cannot perform as promised.

Delegation of responsibilities. In the normal course of business, a listing broker delegates marketing responsibilities to salespeople. An associate may not, however, seek compensation directly from a client. Only the broker can obtain and disburse the compensation.

Causes for termination

A listing may terminate on grounds of:

- performance: all parties perform; the intended outcome
- infeasibility: it is not possible to perform under the terms of the agreement
- mutual agreement: both parties agree to cancel the listing
- revocation: either party cancels the listing, with or without the right
- abandonment: the broker does not attempt to perform
- breach: the terms of the listing are violated
- lapse of time: the listing expires
- invalidity of contract: the listing does not meet the criteria for validity
- incapacitation or death of either party
- involuntary title transfer: condemnation, bankruptcy, foreclosure
- destruction of the property

Listing expiration. In most states, open listings do not require a stated expiration date. Rather, they expire after a "reasonable" period of time as locally defined.

The other types of listing generally must specify a termination date and may not have an automatic renewal mechanism. Courts in many states construe any listing that has no expiration as an open listing.

SOUTH CAROLINA LISTING CONTRACT LANGUAGE AND PROVISIONS

Required contract language

The South Carolina Real Estate Commission requires that certain language be used in all South Carolina listing contracts since January 2017. The required language is as follows:

> *Seller acknowledges receiving an explanation of the types of agency relationships that are offered by brokerage and a South Carolina Disclosure of Real Estate Brokerage Relationships form at the first practical opportunity at which substantive contact occurred between the agent and seller.*
>
> *Seller acknowledges that after entering into this written agency contract, agent might request a modification in order to act as a dual agent or a designated agent in a specific transaction. If asked:*
>
> - *permission to act as a dual agent will not be considered.*
> - *permission to act as a dual agent may be considered at the time I am provided with information about the other party to a transaction. If I agree, I will execute a separate written Dual Agency Agreement.*
> - *permission to act as a designated agent will not be considered.*
> - *permission to act as a designated agent may be considered at the time I am provided with information about the other party to a transaction. If I agree, I will execute a separate written Designated Agency Agreement.*

South Carolina listing provisions

Consent to disclosed dual agency/designated agency. As mentioned above, South Carolina requires specific language in this section and the seller must initial all applicable choices.

Compensation to other agents. The owner authorizes the broker to cooperate and pay compensation to other agents. If there will be no compensation to other agents, the property cannot be listed in the multiple listing service.

Terms. The agreed upon listing price is recorded in this section along with the compensation the broker will receive.

Earnest money. The owner authorizes and designates an escrow agent to hold the earnest money deposit.

Signs. Owner gives permission for the display of signs on the property, relating to its sale.

Broker's duty. Broker agrees to best efforts of agents and staff in procuring a buyer.

Broker liability limitation. This provision explains the limits of the broker's liability to the owner with regard to acts of omission, negligence, misrepresentation, or breach of undertaking, except if the acts were intentional or willful.

Owners' duty. This section lists the owner's obligations to the broker, including such items as furnishing complete and reliable information, allowing inspections and property showings, permitting the broker to take photographs, conveying marketable title to the property, and authorizing the attorneys to provide a copy of the settlement statement to the broker prior to closing.

Property disclosure statement. Owner warrants that there are no material defects that have not been disclosed and that the owner has reviewed and completed a Seller's Property Disclosure Statement.

Disclosure. Broker is authorized to disclose information about the property to agents, subagents, and prospective buyers.

Taxes. Owner agrees to comply with South Carolina withholding requirements for nonresident owners.

Coastal Tidelands & Wetlands Act. Statement that an addendum will be attached if the property is affected by the provisions of this Act.

Multiple listing service. This section indicates whether or not the property will be listed with a multiple listing service.

Lockbox. The owner agrees to lockbox installation or not.

Internet marketing. The owner agrees that the listing may be placed in electronic marketing media or not.

Other offers. The broker's responsibility to present offers ends at the property's closing or at the expiration of the listing agreement.

Marketing the property. The broker will end marketing efforts once an offer has been accepted, unless requested to continue in writing.

No control of commission rates or fees. Compensation for services is negotiated between broker and client and is not controlled, recommended, suggested or maintained by a Board, MLS, or any person not a party to the listing agreement.

Maintenance. Owner will maintain the property until date of closing or possession.

Agreement to sell. Owner agrees to enter into a written sales agreement with a buyer.

Lead-based paint. Appropriate disclosure will be signed and attached to the agreement for any property with a dwelling built before 1978.

Mediation clause. Any dispute or claim resulting from a breach of the agreement or services provided will go to mediation. This clause survives for 120 days after the closing date.

Fair housing. Property is offered in full compliance with fair housing laws.

Enforcement. Broker may take action to enforce the agreement or collect costs, fees, and damages.

SNAPSHOT REVIEW:

Unit 5: LISTING AGREEMENTS

TYPES OF LISTINGS

- owner listing authorizes broker to represent owner or landlord
- 3 types of owner listings: exclusive right-to-sell (or lease); exclusive agency; open listing
- buyer agency or tenant representation agreement authorizes broker to represent buyer or tenant

Exclusive right-to-sell listing

- exclusive authorization-to-sell
- seller contracts exclusively with single broker to procure buyer in exchange of commission

Exclusive agency

- authorizes single broker to sell property and earn commission but leaves owner right to sell property without broker's assistance

Open listing

- on-exclusive authorization to sell or lease property
- multiple brokers can be working with seller

Net listing

- owner sets minimum acceptable amount to be received and allows broker to have any amount in excess as commission

Buyer and tenant agency agreements

- create fiduciary relationship with buyer or tenant
- **Duties of the agent.** Duty to explain how buyer or tenant agency relationships work; diligently locate property that meets requirements; comply with state agency-disclosure laws

Transaction broker agreement

- non-agency relationship with seller or buyer
- agent not bound by fiduciary duties
- binds principal to compensation agreement if broker procures property or buyer

FULFILLMENT AND TERMINATION OF THE LISTING

- agent performs listing agreement by achieving result specified in agreement

Agent's performance

- **Specific responsibilities.** Listing agreement authorizes broker to undertake relevant actions including showing property; locating buyer/seller/tenant/landlord; communicating client's transaction terms, etc.

- **Due diligence.** Verifying accuracy of statements in listing regarding property, owner, owner's representations
- **Delegation of responsibilities.** Listing broker delegates marketing responsibilities to salespeople; only broker can obtain and disburse compensation

Causes for termination

- Performance; infeasibility; mutual agreement; revocation; abandonment; breach; lapse of time; invalidity of contract; incapacitation or death; involuntary title transfer; destruction of property
- **Listing expiration.** Open listings do not require state expiration date; other listing types require specific termination date

SOUTH CAROLINA LISTING CONTRACT LANGUAGE AND PROVISIONS
Required contract language

- SC Real Estate Commission requires certain language in listing contracts

South Carolina listing provisions

- **Consent to disclosed dual agency/designated agency.** Seller must initial all applicable choices
- **Compensation to other agents.** Owner authorizes broker to cooperate and pay compensation to other agents
- **Terms.** Agreed upon listing price and broker compensation
- **Earnest money.** Owner authorizes and designates escrow agent to hold earnest money deposit
- **Signs.** Owner gives permission for signs on property
- **Broker's duty.** Broker agrees to best efforts of agents and staff in procuring buyer
- **Broker liability limitation.** With regards to acts of omission, negligence, misrepresentation, breach of undertaking
- **Owners' duty.** Owner's obligation to broker; furnishing complete and reliable information, allowing inspections and property showings, permitting broker to take photographs, conveying marketable title to property
- **Property disclosure statement.** Owner warrants there are no material defects
- **Disclosure.** Broker authorized to disclose information about property to agents, subagents, and prospective buyers
- **Taxes.** Owner to comply with SC withholding requirements for nonresident owners
- **Coastal Tidelands & Wetlands Act.** Addendum attached if property affected by Act
- **Multiple listing service.** Indicates whether property listed with multiple listing service
- **Lockbox.** Owner agrees to lockbox installation
- **Internet marketing.** Owner agrees to electronic marketing media
- **Other offers.** Broker's responsibility to present offers ends at property's closing or listing agreement expiration
- **Marketing the property.** Broker ends marketing efforts once offer accepted
- **No control of commission rates or fees.** Compensation negotiated between broker and client
- **Maintenance.** Owner maintains property until date of closing
- **Agreement to sell.** Owner agrees to enter written sales agreement
- **Lead-based paint.** Disclosure for property built before 1978
- **Mediation clause.** Dispute or claim resulting from breach of agreement
- **Fair housing. Property in full compliance with fair housing laws**
- **Enforcement.** Broker may enforce agreement or collect costs, fees, damages

==

Check Your Understanding Quiz:

Unit 5: Listing Agreements

Carefully read each question and provide your best answer based on what you learned in this module. Then check your answers against the Answer Key which immediately follows the quiz questions.

1. Which type of listing is rarely used today?

   a. Open listing
   b. Exclusive right-to-sell
   c. Net listing
   d. Exclusive agency

2. Which type of listing is a non-exclusive authorization to lease a property?

   a. Open listing
   b. Net listing
   c. Non-exclusive right-to-lease
   d. Right-to-lease

3. A transaction broker is _____.

   a. in an agency relationship with the seller.
   b. not bound by fiduciary duties to either party.
   c. bound by fiduciary duties to the buyer.
   d. in an agency relationship with the buyer.

4. Michael sells a property for $450,000 but the seller only wanted $375,000. Since Michael is in a(n) _____ agreement with the seller, he ends up keeping $75,000 as commission.

   a. exclusive right-to-sell
   b. open listing
   c. exclusive agency
   d. net listing

5. If a buyer is procured during the listing period of a(n) _____ listing, the broker is entitled to a commission, regardless of who is procuring cause.

   a. exclusive agency
   b. exclusive right-to-sell
   c. open
   d. Procuring cause always matters when it comes to disbursing commissions.

6. What is the most common agreement between brokers and buyers?

    a. Exclusive right-to-represent
    b. Multiple listing agreement
    c. Tenant representation agreement
    d. Net listing agreement

Exercise Workshop -- Unit 5: Listing Agreements

Exercise 5-1. Procuring Cause

Synopsis:

In this exercise, you will be a member of an arbitration panel and determine which party is procuring cause to the sale.

Instructions:

1. Carefully read the case below.
2. Answer the questions that follow.
3. Compare your answers to those listed under the discussion section.

Scenario:

Elizabeth took a listing on a house and placed the listing in the MLS and on Zillow. She received a call from Jay that he would like to look at the house. Elizabeth met Jay at the house and let him in. He wandered around the house then went back outside where Elizabeth was waiting. Elizabeth asked Jay if he had been pre-approved by a lender, and Jay answered no. Elizabeth told Jay he needed to get the loan pre-approval before they could talk about the house.

The next day, Jay called Elizabeth back and asked if he could show the home to his wife. Elizabeth agreed to show them the house. She met them at the house and unlocked the door to let them in. Elizbeth stayed outside and watched their children. When they came out, she again asked if they had been pre-approved for a loan, and they answered no. She again stated that they needed to get loan pre-approval before they could talk about the house.

Jay and his wife went home and called Chris. Chris had been their real estate agent in the past and spoke their language. Jay told Chris about looking at the house Elizabeth had listed and that he and his wife wanted to put in an offer. Chris asked if they had told Elizabeth that they already had a real estate agent, and Jay told him no, she had never asked. He went on to tell Chris that the only thing Elizabeth was interested in was if they were pre-approved for a loan. Jay then told Chris that he had intended to use Chris as his real estate agent all along.

Chris wrote up an offer and submitted it to Elizabeth. The seller accepted the offer and the house closed per the terms of the contract.

After closing, Elizabeth contacted Chris and told him that she felt she was procuring cause of the sale and should receive the commission. She stated that she had not said anything earlier because she did not want to delay the closing. Chris stated that she was not procuring cause, that he was. Elizabeth filed a grievance with her local association of Realtors, and the case was sent to an arbitration panel.

REMEMBER: In arbitration, there is a winner and a loser. The panel can't decide that the money should be split among the parties. Also, note that in this case, Chris and his company made several offers to share the commission, but Elizabeth insisted that she was procuring cause and thus should get all of the money.

Questions:

1. What is procuring cause?

2. Who do you believe is procuring cause in this case? Why?

Exercise Workshop -- Unit 5: Listing Agreement

Exercise 5-2. Completing a Listing Agreement

Synopsis:

In this exercise, you will identify the various types of Listing Agreements used in real estate transactions.

Instructions:

In the first exercise, match the type of listing agreement with the scenario presented. In the second exercise, match the term to the definition.

Exercise 1:

- A. Open Listing
- B. Exclusive Right of Sale Listing
- C. Net Listing
- D. Exclusive Agency Listing
- E. Multiple Listing

_____ 1. Ron tells his real estate agent he needs to clear $150,000 for the sale of his home. Anything the agent can get over that amount will be the agent's commission.

_____ 2. Rachel takes a listing where she gets paid no matter who brings in the house's buyer during the listing agreement's timeframe.

_____ 3. Charlie lists a house and puts it in MLS. The agreement states that if Charlie locates the buyer, he will earn the commission; however, the house owner can sell the house herself and not pay Charlie a commission.

_____ 4. Martina comes to a real estate broker's meeting and announces that she will pay a 3% commission to any brokerage that can sell her house.

_____ 5. Only Exclusive Right of Sale Listings and Exclusive Agency Listing is allowed to be posted. The post must list the amount to be paid to an agent who brings in the property buyer.

Exercise 2:

    A. Effect a sale
    B. Find a buyer
    C. Time is of the essence
    D. Due diligence
    E. Termination of listing

_____ 1. Includes destruction of property, incapacitation of any party, death, breach & performance as ways of getting out of a listing agreement.

_____ 2. The agent must locate a person who is ready, willing, and able to buy the house to earn their commission.

_____ 3. The contract must have expiration dates in the contract, and all parties must meet these deadlines.

_____ 4. A broker or agent must verify the accuracy of the owner's statements regarding the property's condition.

_____ 5. The agent must locate a person who is ready, willing, and able to buy the house but must see the contract through to closing.

Unit 6: Purchase and Sale Contracts

Unit 6: Purchase and Sale Contracts – Learning Objectives

When the student has completed Unit 6, he or she will be able to:

> **1. Characterize the central provisions of South Carolina purchase and sale contracts and the licensee's role in completing such agreements**
>
> **2 Describe how licensees can properly avoid the unauthorized practice of law with respect to contract completion**

LEGAL CHARACTERISTICS

Overview

A real estate sale contract is a binding and enforceable agreement wherein a buyer, the vendee, agrees to buy an identified parcel of real estate, and a seller, the vendor, agrees to sell it under certain terms and conditions. It is the document that is at the center of the transaction.

The conventional transfer of real estate ownership takes place in three stages. First, there is the negotiating period where buyers and sellers exchange offers in an effort to agree to all transfer terms that will appear in the sale contract. Second, when both parties have accepted all terms, the offer becomes a binding sale contract and the transaction enters the pre-closing stage, during which each party makes arrangements to complete the sale according to the sale contract's terms. Third is the closing of the transaction, when the seller deeds title to the buyer, the buyer pays the purchase price, and all necessary documents are completed. At this stage, the sale contract has served its purpose and terminates.

Other names for the sale contract are *agreement of sale, contract for purchase, contract of purchase and sale, and earnest money contract*.

Executory contract. A sale contract is executory: the signatories have yet to perform their respective obligations and promises. Upon closing, the sale contract is fully performed and no longer exists as a binding agreement.

Signatures. All owners of the property should sign the sale contract. If the sellers are married, both spouses should sign to ensure that both spouses release homestead, dower, and curtesy rights to the buyer at closing. Failure to do so does not invalidate the contract but can lead to encumbered title and legal disputes.

Contract enforceability

To be enforceable, a sale contract must:

- be validly created (mutual consent, consideration, legal purpose, competent parties, voluntary act)
- be in writing
- identify the principal parties
- clearly identify the property, preferably by legal description
- contain a purchase price
- be signed by the principal parties

Written vs. oral form. A contract for the sale of real estate is enforceable only if it is in writing. A buyer or seller cannot sue to force the other to comply with an oral contract for sale, even if the contract is valid.

Assignment. Either party to a sale transaction can assign the sale contract to another party, subject to the provisions and conditions contained in the agreement.

Who may complete. A broker or agent may assist the buyer and seller in completing an offer to purchase, provided the broker represents the client faithfully and does not charge a separate fee for the assistance. It is advisable, and legally required in most states, for a broker to use a standard contract form promulgated by state agencies or real estate boards, as such forms contain generally accepted language. This relieves the broker of the dangers of creating new contract language, which can be construed as a practice of law for which the broker is not licensed.

Contract creation

Offer and acceptance. A contract of sale is created by full and unequivocal acceptance of an offer. Offer and acceptance may come from either buyer or seller. The offeree must accept the offer without making any changes whatsoever. A change terminates the offer and creates a new offer, or counteroffer. An offeror may revoke an offer for any reason prior to communication of acceptance by the offeree. Equitable title. A sale contract gives the buyer an interest in the property that is called equitable title, or ownership in equity. If the seller defaults and the buyer can show good faith performance, the buyer can sue for specific performance, that is, to compel the seller to transfer legal title upon payment of the contract price.

Earnest money escrow

The buyer's earnest money deposit fulfills the consideration requirements for a valid sale contract. In addition, it provides potential compensation for damages to the seller if the buyer fails to perform. The amount of the deposit varies according to local custom. It should be noted that the earnest money deposit is not the only form of consideration that satisfies the requirement.

The sale contract provides the escrow instructions for handling and disbursing escrow funds. The earnest money is placed in a third-party trust account or escrow. A licensed escrow agent employed by a title company, financial institution, or brokerage company usually manages the escrow. An individual broker may also serve as the escrow agent.

The escrow holder acts as an impartial fiduciary for buyer and seller. If the buyer performs under the sale contract, the deposit is applied to the purchase price.

Strict rules govern the handling of earnest money deposits, particularly if a broker is the escrow agent. For example, state laws direct the broker when to deposit the funds, how to account for them, and how to keep them separate from the broker's own funds.

Contract contingencies

A sale contract often contains contingencies. A contingency is a condition that must be met before the contract is enforceable.

Financing contingency. The most common contingency concerns financing. A buyer makes an offer contingent upon securing financing for the property under certain terms on or before a certain date. If unable to secure the specified loan commitment by the deadline, the buyer may cancel the contract and recover the deposit. An appropriate and timely loan commitment eliminates the contingency, and the buyer must proceed with the purchase.

It is possible for both buyers and sellers to abuse contingencies in order to leave themselves a convenient way to cancel without defaulting. To avoid problems, the statement of a contingency should:

- be explicit and clear
- have an expiration date
- expressly require diligence in the effort to fulfill the requirement

A contingency that is too broad, vague, or excessive in duration may invalidate the entire contract on the grounds of insufficiency of mutual agreement.

Default

A sale contract is bilateral, since both parties promise to perform. As a result, either party may default by failing to perform. Note that a party's failure to meet a contingency does not constitute default, but rather entitles the parties to cancel the contract.

Buyer default. If a buyer fails to perform under the terms of a sale contract, the breach entitles the seller to legal recourse for damages. In most cases, the contract itself stipulates the seller's remedies. The usual remedy is forfeiture of the buyer's deposit as **liquidated damages**, provided the deposit is not grossly in excess of the seller's actual damages. It is also customary to provide for the seller and broker to share the liquidated damages. The broker may not, however, receive liquidated damages in excess of what the commission would have been on the full listing price.

If the contract does not provide for liquidated damages, the seller may sue for damages, cancellation, or specific performance.

Seller default. If a seller defaults, the buyer may sue for specific performance, damages, or cancellation.

SOUTH CAROLINA OFFERS TO PURCHASE

Contracting procedures

When dealing with offers to purchase property, licensees must

- prepare all offers in writing when received and promptly present them to the seller
- quickly deliver true, executed copies of a written acceptance of an offer to all parties as soon as obtained
- ensure that all of the terms and conditions of the transaction are included in the offer
- ensure that changes or modifications made during negotiation are in writing and initialed and dated by both parties before continuing with the transaction

Unauthorized practice of law. Licensees may complete sales contracts by filling in form blanks as directed by the client or customer. However, licensees are considered to be practicing law without a license if they create contract provisions using their own wording. Caution is therefore well-advised when completing the written sales contract form.

What contract form to use. Licensees are strongly advised to restrict usage of contract forms to those adopted by the firm or those promulgated by the state or by the local board of Realtors®. The benefit of using forms is that the form's language is typically accepted practice which insulates the licensee from exposure to creating problematic contracts or practicing law without a license.

Rejected offers without a counter. If an offer is rejected without a counter, the licensee must sign the Commission-**promulgated Real Estate Offer Rejection Form** which affirms presentation of the offer. The licensee must provide this form to the offeror within 48 hours, whether the licensee is the agent of the buyer or the seller or is acting as a transaction broker.

Electronic communication of offers. A licensee may communicate an offer and/or counteroffer by fax or other secure electronic means including the Internet. The signatures, initials, and handwritten or typewritten modifications on those electronic documents are considered as valid and binding on the parties as the signatures, initials, and other modifications on the original hard-copy documents would be.

Buyer/seller acknowledgements. The bottom of each page of the agreement has spaces for all buyers and sellers to initial that they "have read this page."

South Carolina sales contract provisions and considerations

Parties, consideration, and property. One or more clauses will identify the parties, the property, and the basic consideration, which is the sale of the property in return for a purchase price.

There must be at least two parties to a sale contract: one cannot convey property to oneself. All parties must be identified, be of legal age, and have the capacity to contract.

The property clause contains the legal identification of the property. This provision also identifies fixtures and personal property included in the sale. Unless expressly excluded, items commonly construed as fixtures are included in the sale. Similarly, items commonly considered personal property are not included unless expressly included.

Price and terms. This clause states the final price and details how the purchase will occur. Of particular interest to the seller is the buyer's down payment, since the greater the buyer's equity, the more likely the buyer will be able to secure financing. In addition, a large deposit represents a buyer's commitment to complete the sale.

If seller financing is involved, this provision sets forth the terms of the arrangement: the amount and type of loan, the rate and term, and how the loan will be paid off. It is important for all parties to verify that the buyer's earnest money deposit, down payment, loan proceeds, and other promised funds together equal the purchase price stated in the contract.

Earnest money deposit. These provisions specify how the buyer will pay the earnest money. It may allow the buyer to pay it in installments or all at once. The former option enables a buyer to hold on to the property briefly while obtaining the additional deposit funds. For example, a buyer who wants to buy a house makes an initial deposit of $200, to be followed in twenty-four hours with an additional $2,000. The sale contract includes the seller's acknowledgment of receipt of the deposit.

Closing and possession dates. This provision states when title will transfer, as well as when the buyer will take physical possession. Customarily, possession occurs on the date when the deed is recorded, unless the buyer has agreed to other arrangements.

The closing clause generally describes what must take place at closing to avoid default. A seller must provide clear and marketable title. A buyer must produce purchase funds. Failure to complete any pre-closing requirements stated in the sale contract is default and grounds for the aggrieved party to seek recourse.

Time is of the essence. This provision introduces the requirement that certain deadlines must be met or else the party who fails to act in a timely manner is in default. This in turn enables the other party to opt out of the contract.

Conveyed interest; type of deed. One or more provisions in the contract will state what type of deed the seller will use to convey the property, and what conditions the deed will be subject to. Among common "subject to" conditions are easements, association memberships, encumbrances, mortgages, liens, and special assessments. Typically, the seller conveys a fee simple interest by means of a general warranty deed.

Title evidence. The seller covenants to produce the best possible evidence of property ownership. This is commonly in the form of title insurance. Also implied here is that the seller is conveying marketable title, meaning free and clear of clouds, liens and other encumbrances on title.

Damage and destruction. This provision stipulates the obligations of the parties in case the property is damaged or destroyed during the pre-closing period. Here, the parties may negotiate alternatives including whose obligation it is to repair, and the buyer's obligation to buy if repairs are made. Finally, the clause may provide the option for either party to cancel.

Repair procedure. The South Carolina agreement has a very detailed set of paragraphs dealing with an agreed upon repair procedure. The contract states that the parties agree to the procedure outlined, unless a Due Diligence Addendum is agreed upon and attached to the contract.

Appraised value. This paragraph is the place to indicate by a checkmark whether or not the contract is contingent upon the lender's appraisal.

Default. Here, the contract specifies what constitutes default and what remedies are available for the damaged party. These are basically threefold: specific performance, liquidated damages, or a lawsuit. Specific performance is typically a buyer's remedy for a defaulting seller. Here, the court orders the defaulting party to comply with the terms of the agreement. Liquidated damages is basically the buyer's forfeiture of the deposit in the event the buyer defaults on a given term. Thirdly, either party can file a lawsuit for damages which can vary depending on the case.

Covenants and conditions disclosure. The sales contract should disclose or make reference to the existence of any restrictions imposed on the property by prior owners or by any homeowners association.

C.L.U.E. Report. The CLUE report (Comprehensive Loss Underwriting Exchange) is a claims history database used by insurance companies in underwriting or rating insurance policies. A CLUE Home Seller's Disclosure Report shows a five-year insurance loss history for a specific property. Among other things, it describes the types of any losses and the amounts paid. Many home buyers now require sellers to provide a CLUE Report as a contingency appended to the purchase offer.

Mediation. This provision explains mediation as an alternative dispute resolution system and explains that participants voluntarily decide the settlement terms with the help of a mediator. The provision further states that any dispute relating to the contract will be submitted to mediation.

Transaction information. Although not technically a provision, most South Carolina purchase contracts include a page that contains transactional information, including

- escrow agent name, contact information, and signature
- licensee and brokerage information for both the listing and selling sides
- type of agency representation each broker is providing
- a note about designated agency which states that the broker-in-charge and all supervised licensees, except the designated agents, are dual agents.

SNAPSHOT REVIEW:

Unit 6: PURCHASE AND SALE CONTRACTS

LEGAL CHARACTERISTICS
Overview

- real estate sale contract is binding and enforceable
- 3 stages of real estate ownership transfer: negotiation; pre-closing state; closing
- **Executory contract.** Signatories have yet to perform respective obligations and promises
- **Signatures.** All owners of property should sign sale contract

Contract enforceability

- sale contract must be validly created; in writing; identify principal parties, property, purchase price; be signed by all parties
- **Written vs. oral form.** Contract must be in writing
- **Assignment.** Either party can assign sale contract to another party
- **Who may complete. B**roker or agent may assist buyer and seller in completing offer

Contract creation

- **Offer and acceptance.** Contract created by full and unequivocal acceptance of offer

Earnest money escrow

- fulfills consideration requirements for valid sale contract
- potential compensation for damages to seller if buyer fails to perform
- placed in third party trust account or escrow

Contract contingencies

- **Financing contingency.** Buyer may cancel contract and recover deposit if unable to secure loan commitment by deadline

Default

- **Buyer default.** If buyer fails to perform, seller entitled to legal recourse for damages and buyer's deposit
- **Seller default.** If seller defaults, buyer may sue for specific performance, damages, cancellation

SOUTH CAROLINA OFFERS TO PURCHASE

- **Contracting procedures.** Prepare offers in writing; deliver executed copies; ensure all terms and conditions included; ensure changes or modifications are initialed and dated
- **Unauthorized practice of law.** Licensees considered practicing law without license if create contract provisions with own wording
- **What contract form to use.** Forms promulgated by state or local board of Realtors®

- **Rejected offers without counter.** Licensee must sign Commission-promulgated Real Estate Offer Rejection Form which affirms presentation of offer; this form must be submitted to offeror within 48 hours
- **Electronic communication of offers.** Licensee may communicate offer/counteroffer by fax or Internet
- **Buyer/seller acknowledgements.** Bottom of each agreement page must be initialed by buyers and sellers

South Carolina sales contract provisions and considerations

- **Parties, consideration and property.** Need 2 parties; property clause needs legal identification
- **Price and terms.** Final price and details on how purchase will occur
- **Earnest money deposit.** Specify how buyer pays earnest money
- **Closing and possession dates.** When title will transfer and when buyer will take possession
- **Time is of the essence.** Deadlines must be met or party who fails to act in timely manner is in default
- **Conveyed interest; type of deed.** Type of deed seller uses to convey property
- **Title evidence.** Seller covenants to produce best possible evidence of property ownership
- **Damage and destruction.** Stipulates obligations of parties in case property is damaged or destroyed during pre-closing period
- **Repair procedure.** Parties agree to repair procedure unless a Due Diligence Addendum is attached
- **Appraised value.** Indicate whether contract contingent on appraisal
- **Default.** What constitutes default and what remedies available for damaged party
- **Covenants and conditions disclosure.** Sales contract should disclose or make reference to existence of restrictions imposed on property by prior owners or any homeowners association
- **C.L.U.E. Report.** Claims history database used by insurance companies in underwriting or rating insurance policies
- **Mediation.** Explains mediation as alternative dispute resolution system; participants voluntarily decide settlement terms with mediator help
- **Transaction information.** Escrow agent name and contact information; licensee and brokerage information; type of agency representation; broker-in-charge and all supervised licensees are dual agents.

===

Check Your Understanding Quiz:

Unit 6: Purchase and Sale Contracts

Carefully read each question and provide your best answer based on what you learned in this module. Then check your answers against the Answer Key which immediately follows the quiz questions.

1. How much is a typical earnest money deposit?

    a. $1,000
    b. 3% of the purchase price
    c. $6,000
    d. It varies according to local custom.

2. What is the most common contract contingency?

    a. Financing contingency
    b. Appraisal contingency
    c. Lead-based paint contingency
    d. Property disclosure contingency

3. What is the most common remedy for a buyer default?

    a. Lawsuit for specific performance
    b. Jail time
    c. Forfeiture of buyer's deposit as liquidated damages
    d. A fine paid to the multiple listing service

4. If the signatories of a contract have yet to perform their respective obligations, then the sale contract is _____.

    a. validated.
    b. executory.
    c. enforced.
    d. completed.

5. What is the first stage in the transfer of real estate ownership?

    a. Pre-closing stage
    b. Transferring period
    c. Negotiating period
    d. Binding stage

6. A sale contract gives the buyer an interest in the property that is called _____.

    a. equitable title.
    b. contracted deed.
    c. promissory note.
    d. transferrable equity.

7. If an offer is rejected without a counter, the licensee must ____ _____.

    a. send notice to the local MLS.
    b. sign and submit the Real Estate Offer Rejection Form within 48 hours.
    c. have the buyer sign the Contract Rejection Form.
    d. Nothing is required of the licensee.

==

Exercise Workshop -- Unit 6: Purchase and Sale Contracts

Exercise 6-1. Contract Creation

Synopsis:

In this exercise, the student identifies and defines key provisions of the South Caroline Purchase and Sale Contract.

Instructions:

Match the terms with the description of how the term is used in the Purchase and Sale Contract.

Exercise:

    A. Executory contract
    B. Enforceability
    C. Assignment
    D. Contingencies
    E. Earnest money deposit
    F. Default
    G. Consideration
    H. Time is of the essence

_____ 1. A condition that must be met before the contract is enforceable. Common types are financing, inspection, and appraisals.

_____ 2. A contract with all of the legally required elements, including being in writing, being validly created, identifying the parties, states the consideration and is signed by all parties.

_____ 3. One party fails to meet their obligations under the contract.

_____ 4. All parties have signed the contract but have not fulfilled their obligations and promises.

_____ 5. Money that is given as consideration in the formation of the contract. It may serve as liquidated damages if one party defaults on the contract.

_____ 6. The contract has set deadlines for which contingencies and promises must be met.

_____ 7. The contract can be given or sold to a third party who must meet all the provisions and promises made in the contract.

_____ 8. The deed to the property in exchange for a specific amount of money.

Exercise Workshop -- Unit 6: Purchase and Sale Contract

Exercise 6-2. Contract Creation

Synopsis:

In this exercise, the student will demonstrate their knowledge of the information needed in a contract and demonstrate their ability to complete a Purchase and Sales Contract correctly.

Instructions:

Use the scenario below to complete the sample contract on the next page. Then compare your contract with the contract presented following the exercise.

Scenario:

Gloria and Stephen Grigsby, husband, and wife, are working with Realtor Olivia to find a new home. They found a house with three bedrooms and three baths in a neighborhood they like listed for $185,000. The home is in a community with an HOA with a monthly payment of $100. After looking at the house, they decide to put in an offer.

They agree to give Olivia a check for $5,000 as an escrow deposit. They are pre-approved for a conventional mortgage loan from their bank up to $150,000 and will pay cash for the remaining balance. They do not want to pay any more than 4% APR on the mortgage and want that financial contingency inserted into the contract.

After looking at the public records, Olivia finds the following information: Current owners of the home are Mark and Dawn Spencer, husband and wife. The house is located at 1436 Highland Road, Columbia, SC 29000 in Richland County. The Property Tax ID number is R1234-12-21. The legal description is Block 12, Lot C of Richmond Heights Subdivision, as recorded in the county records of Richland County. Records show the house was built in 1974.

John's Title will hold the escrow deposit and handle the closing. John's Title is located at 321 Anywhere Road, Columbia, SC 29000. Phone number is 800-555-4321, and the email is JTitle@gmail.com.

The Grigsby's ask that the Refrigerator, range, dishwasher, and fixtures convey with the house. They have also requested Olivia to put in an appraisal contingency.

Olivia is giving the seller until June 13, 2022, to accept, deny or counter their offer. An except closing to be on or before August 1, 2022.

REMEMBER: The essential part of completing a contract is not to leave any blanks.

Purchase and Sale Contract for Residential Real Estate

PARTIES: _____ _____(Seller) and
_____(Buyer)

Agree to sell and convey real and personal property as described below.

PROPERTY DESCRIPTION:

Street Address: _____

Located in: _____ County, South Carolina. Tax ID: _____

Real Property: Legal Description:

_____

_____

Personal Property: _____

_____

Purchase Price:...$_____

Escrow Deposit (_) accompanies offer or (_) due with _____ days ..$ _____

Escrow Agent Information: Name _____

Address: _____

Phone: _____ Email: _____

Financing: Express as dollar amount or percentage $ _____

(_) Conventional (_) FHA (_) VA (_) Owner Financing   APR% _____

Cash to Close $_____

Time to Accept Offer and Count-Offer: _____

Closing Date: _____

ADDENDA ADDED: _____

ADDITIONAL TERMS: _____

_____   _____
Buyer's Signature   Seller's Signature

Unit 7: Option-to-buy Contracts

Unit 7: Option-to-buy Contracts – Learning Objectives

When the student has completed Unit 7, he or she will be able to:

1. Describe the essential requirements of a valid option-to-purchase contract and its central provisions

OVERVIEW

An option-to-buy is an enforceable contract in which a potential seller, the **optionor**, grants a potential buyer, the **optionee**, the right to purchase a property before a stated time for a stated price and terms. In exchange for the right of option, the optionee pays the optionor valuable consideration.

For example, a buyer wants to purchase a property for $350,000, but needs to sell a boat to raise the down payment. The boat will take two or three months to sell. To accommodate the buyer, the seller offers the buyer an option to purchase the property at any time before midnight on the day that is ninety days from the date of signing the option. The buyer pays the seller $1,000 for the option. If buyer exercises the option, the seller will apply the $1,000 toward the earnest money deposit and subsequent down payment. If the optionee lets the option expire, the seller keeps the $1,000. Both parties agree to the arrangement by completing a sale contract as an addendum to the option, then executing the option agreement itself.

An option-to-buy places the optionee under no obligation to purchase the property. However, the seller must perform under the terms of the contract if the buyer exercises the option. An option is thus a unilateral agreement. Exercise of the option creates a bilateral sale contract where both parties are bound to perform. An unused option terminates at the expiration date.

An optionee can use an option to prevent the sale of a property to another party while seeking to raise funds for the purchase. A renter with a lease option-to-buy can accumulate down payment funds while paying rent to the landlord. For example, an owner may lease a condominium to a tenant with an option to buy. If the tenant takes the option, the landlord agrees to apply $100 of the monthly rent paid prior to the option date toward the purchase price. The tenant pays the landlord the nominal sum of $200 for the option.

Options can also facilitate commercial property acquisition. The option period gives a buyer time to investigate zoning, space planning, building permits, environmental impacts, and other feasibility issues prior to the purchase without losing the property to another party in the meantime.

CONTRACT REQUIREMENTS

To be valid and enforceable, an option-to-buy must:

- include actual, non-refundable consideration

  The option must require the optionee to pay a specific consideration that is separate from the purchase price. The consideration cannot be refunded if the option is not exercised. If the option is exercised, the consideration may be applied to the purchase price. If the option is a lease option, portions of the rent may qualify as separate consideration.

- include price and terms of the sale

  The price and terms of the potential transaction must be clearly expressed and cannot change over the option period. It is customary practice for the parties to complete and attach a sale contract to the option as satisfaction of this requirement.

- have an expiration date

  The option must automatically expire at the end of a specific period.

- be in writing

  Since a potential transfer of real estate is involved, most state statutes of fraud require an option to be in writing.

- include a legal description

- meet general contract validity requirements

  The basics include competent parties, the optionor's promise to perform, and the optionor's signature. Note that it is not necessary for the optionee to sign the option.

Legal issues

Equitable interest. The optionee enjoys an equitable interest in the property because the option creates the right to obtain legal title. However, the option does not in itself convey an interest in real property, only a right to do something governed by contract law.

Recording. An option should be recorded, because the equitable interest it creates can affect the marketability of title.

Assignment. An option-to-buy is assignable unless the contract expressly prohibits assignment.

RIGHT OF FIRST REFUSAL

A right of first refusal granted by a seller to a buyer gives the buyer a "right" to buy the seller's property should he or she desire to do so within an agreed upon time parameter and for a given price. In effect a right of first refusal gives a person an option that may or may not be exercised by the option holder.

In practice the right of first refusal is an informal and not necessarily enforceable agreement between an owner and a buyer. Generally there are too many unspecified details in the agreement to make it "leak proof" enough to enforce. Key issues such as price, timing, duration of the agreement, etc. make these agreements untenable at best in a court of law.

SNAPSHOT REVIEW:

Unit 7: OPTION-TO-BUY CONTRACTS

OVERVIEW

- seller (optionor) grants potential buyer (optionee) right to purchase property before a stated time for a stated price and terms
- optionee pays optionor
- option-to-buy places optionee under no obligation to purchase property

CONTRACT REQUIREMENTS

- include actual, non-refundable consideration; price and terms of sale; expiration date; be in writing; legal description; general contract validity requirements

Legal issues

- **Equitable interest.** Option creates right to obtain legal title
- **Recording.** Option should be recorded
- **Assignment.** Option-to-buy is assignable unless stated otherwise

RIGHT OF FIRST REFUSAL

- granted by seller to buyer to give buyer "right" to buy seller's property should he or she desire to do so within agreed upon time parameter for given price
- informal and not necessarily enforceable

==

Check Your Understanding Quiz:

Unit 7: Option-to-buy Contracts

Carefully read each question and provide your best answer based on what you learned in this module. Then check your answers against the Answer Key which immediately follows the quiz questions.

1. Which type of contract grants a buyer the right to purchase a property before a stated time for a stated price and terms?

    a. Rent-to-own contract
    b. Option-to-buy contract
    c. Purchase-lease contract
    d. Seller financed contract

2. The optionee enjoys a(n) _____ the property because the option creates the right to obtain legal title.

    a. equitable interest in
    b. recorded deed on
    c. warrantable deed for
    d. enforced interest in

3. When must an optionee purchase the property they are leasing?

    a. Within 12 months of signing the contract
    b. After 3 years of leasing
    c. An option-to-buy places the optionee under no obligation to purchase the property.
    d. Within 6 months of signing the contract

Unit 8: Contracts for Deed

Unit 8: Contracts for Deed – Learning Objectives

When the student has completed Unit 8, he or she will be able to:

> **1. Describe the salient mechanics of a contract for deed and how this transaction differs from conventional conveyances with respect to enforcement and legal title**

ESSENTIAL FEATURES AND PURPOSE

A contract for deed is also called a *land contract*, an *installment sale*, a *conditional sales contract*, and an *agreement for deed*. It is a bilateral agreement between a seller, the **vendor**, and a buyer, the **vendee**, in which the vendor defers receipt of some or all of the purchase price of a property over a specified period of time. During the period, *the vendor retains legal title* and the vendee acquires equitable title. The vendee takes possession of the property, makes stipulated payments of principal and interest to the vendor, and otherwise fulfills obligations as the contract requires. At the end of the period, the buyer pays the vendor the full purchase price and the vendor deeds legal title to the vendee

Like an option, a contract for deed offers a means for a marginally qualified buyer to acquire property. In essence, the seller acts as lender, allowing the buyer to take possession and pay off the purchase price over time. A buyer may thus avoid conventional down payment and income requirements imposed by institutional lenders. During the contract period, the buyer can work to raise the necessary cash to complete the purchase or to qualify for a conventional mortgage.

A contract for deed serves two primary purposes for a seller. First, it facilitates a sale that might otherwise be impossible. Second, it may give the seller certain tax benefits. Since the seller is not liable for capital gains tax until the purchase price is received, the installment sale lowers the seller's tax liability in the year of the sale.

Rights and obligations of the parties

Vendor's rights and obligations. During the contract period, the seller may:

- mortgage the property
- sell or assign whatever interests he or she owns in the property to another party
- incur judgment liens against the property

The vendor, however, is bound to the obligations imposed by the contract for deed. In particular, the vendor may not breach the obligation to convey legal title to the vendee upon receipt of the total purchase price. In addition, the vendor remains liable for underlying mortgage loans.

Vendee's rights and obligations. During the contract period, the buyer may occupy, use, enjoy, and profit from the property, subject to the provisions of the written agreement. The vendee must make periodic payments of principal and interest and maintain the property. In addition, a vendee may have to pay property taxes and hazard insurance.

Legal form

Like other conveyance contracts, a contract for deed instrument identifies:

- the principal parties
- the property's legal description
- consideration: specifically what the parties promise to do
- the terms of the sale
- obligations for property maintenance
- default and remedies
- signatures and acknowledgment

The contract specifies the vendee's payments, payment deadlines, when the balance of the purchase price is due, and how the property may be used.

Default and recourse

Seller default. If the seller defaults, such as by failing to deliver the deed, the buyer may sue for specific performance, or for cancellation of the agreement and damages.

Buyer default. States differ in the remedies they prescribe for the seller in case of buyer default. Some states consider the default a breach of contract that may be remedied by cancellation, retention of monies received, and eviction. Others provide foreclosure proceedings as a remedy.

MANAGING RISK

Most real estate markets do not have standardized language or uniform provisions for the contract for deed transaction in any form sanctioned by associations and agencies. Therefore, this kind of conveyance presents certain pitfalls and dangers for buyer and seller.

In some states, a breach of the contract for deed is remedied under *local contract law* rather than foreclosure law. Therefore, the buyer may not have the protections of a redemption period or other buyer-protection laws which accompany formal foreclosure proceedings. The vendor might sue the vendee for breach of contract for the slightest infraction of the contract terms.

A second danger for the vendee is that the vendor has the power and the right to encumber the property in ways that may not be desirable for the buyer. For example, the seller could place a home equity loan on the property, then fail to make periodic payments. The bank could then foreclose on the vendor, thus jeopardizing the vendee's eventual purchase.

For the seller, the principal danger is that the buyer acquires possession in exchange for a minimal down payment. A buyer might damage or even vacate the property, leaving the seller to make repairs and retake possession. Further, since the contract is recorded, the seller must also bear the time and expense of clearing the title.

To minimize risk, principal parties in a contract for deed should observe the following guidelines:

- use an attorney to draft the agreement
- adopt the standard forms, if available
- become familiar with how the contract will be enforced
- utilize professional escrow and title services
- record the transaction properly
- be prepared for the possible effect on existing financing

SNAPSHOT REVIEW:

Unit 8: CONTRACTS FOR DEED

ESSENTIAL FEATURES AND PURPOSE

- bilateral agreement between seller (vendor) and buyer (vendee) where vendor defers receipt of some or all of purchase price of property over specified period of time
- vendor retains legal title and vendee acquires equitable title
- vendee takes possession of property, makes stipulated payments to vendor, and fulfills contract
- at end of period, buyer pays vendor full purchase price and vendor deeds legal title to vendee
- seller acts as lender

Rights and obligations of the parties

- **Vendor's rights and obligations.** Seller may mortgage property; sell or assign interests to other party; incur judgment liens against property
- **Vendee's rights and obligations.** Buyer may occupy, use, enjoy profit from property; make periodic payments of principal and interest and maintain property

Legal form

- identifies principal parties; legal description; consideration; terms of sale; property maintenance; default; signatures

Default and recourse

- **Seller default.** Buyer may sue for specific performance, or cancellation of agreement and damages
- **Buyer default.** Cancellation; retention of monies received; eviction; foreclosure

MANAGING RISK

- uncommon to have standardized language or provisions for contract for deed transaction
- to minimize risk: use attorney to draft agreement; adopt standard forms; familiarize with how contract enforced; utilize professional escrow and title services; record transaction properly; be prepared for possible effect on existing financing

==

Check Your Understanding Quiz:

Unit 8: Contracts for Deed

Carefully read each question and provide your best answer based on what you learned in this module. Then check your answers against the Answer Key which immediately follows the quiz questions.

1. During a contract for deed, the _____ retains legal title while the other party acquires equitable title.

   a. vendor
   b. buyer
   c. vendee
   d. listing agent

2. A breach of the contract for deed is remedied under _____ rather than foreclosure law.

   a. real estate law
   b. federal law
   c. local contract law
   d. renting law

3. What payments is a buyer required to make during the contract period?

   a. Property taxes only
   b. Principal, interest, taxes and hazard insurance
   c. Home insurance and principal
   d. Market value rent and interest

4. Which of the following is a responsibility of the vendee?

   a. Mortgage the property
   b. Assign interest to another party
   c. Incur judgment liens against property
   d. Make the agreed upon periodic payments

==

Module C: ETHICS AND REAL ESTATE

Unit 9: Fiduciary Duties
Unit 10: Trust Fund Handling
Unit 11: Regulatory Compliance
Unit 12: Professional Practices

Module C Learning Objectives

Fiduciary Duties

   1. Describe what actions and ethical practices are imposed under the umbrella of 'fiduciary duties' in an agency relationship with the client
   2. Contrast one's duties imposed as ethical practices in brokerage relationships with customers as opposed to clients

Trust Fund Handling

   1. Describe the foundations of ethical practices in the context of managing the trust funds of third parties, with particular respect to timely depositing; reconciliation; proper disbursement; commingling; and conversion

Regulatory Compliance

   1. Demonstrate an awareness of competent practice as it is determined by compliance with brokerage practice laws and regulations

Professional Practices

   1. Explain the critical foundations of fair housing law and ADA compliance with particular respect to anti-discriminatory activities; advertising violations; South Carolina's protected classes; and equal access to public accommodations
   2 Summarize the central purposes and thrusts of the Fair Credit Act; describe the prohibition of redlining
   3. Summarize the illegal practices of blockbusting, collusion, and market allocation, and why such practices are illegal
   4. Generally characterize the purpose, structure and overall thrusts of the Realtors@' Code of Ethics, Pathways to Professionalism and their Commitment to Excellence program
   5. Explain the purpose and general content of a brokerage's policy and procedure's manual as it relates to the broker's duty to supervise and train subordinates

Unit 9: Fiduciary Duties

When the student has completed Unit 9, he or she will be able to:

1. Describe what actions and ethical practices are imposed under the umbrella of 'fiduciary duties' in an agency relationship with the client

2. Contrast one's duties imposed as ethical practices in brokerage relationships with customers as opposed to clients

FIDUCIARY DUTIES

The agency relationship imposes fiduciary duties on the client and agent, but particularly on the agent. An agent must also observe certain standards of conduct in dealing with customers and other outside parties

Agent's duties to the client

Skill, care, and diligence. The agent is hired to do a job, and is therefore expected to do it with diligence and reasonable competence. Competence is generally defined as a level of real estate marketing skills and knowledge comparable to those of other practitioners in the area.

The notion of care extends to observing the limited scope of authority granted to the agent. A conventional listing agreement does not authorize an agent to obligate the client to contracts, and it does not allow the agent to conceal offers to buy, sell, or lease coming from a customer or another agent. Further, since a client relies on a broker's representations, a broker must exercise care not to offer advice outside of his or her field of expertise. Violations of this standard may expose the agent to liability for the unlicensed practice of a profession such as law, engineering, or accounting.

Loyalty. The duty of loyalty requires the agent to place the interests of the client above those of all others, particularly the agent's own. This standard is particularly relevant whenever an agent discusses transaction terms with a prospect.

Obedience. An agent must comply with the client's directions and instructions, provided they are legal. An agent who cannot obey a legal directive, for whatever reason, must withdraw from the relationship. If the directive is illegal, the agent must also immediately withdraw.

Confidentiality. An agent must hold in confidence any personal or business information received from the client during the term of employment. An agent may not disclose any information that would harm the client's interests or bargaining position, or anything else the client wishes to keep secret.
The confidentiality standard is one of the duties that extends beyond the termination of the listing: at no time in the future may the agent disclose confidential information.

An agent must exercise care in fulfilling this duty: if confidentiality conflicts with the agent's legal requirements to disclose material facts, the agent must inform the client of this obligation and make the required disclosures. If such a conflict cannot be resolved, the agent must withdraw from the relationship.

Accounting. An agent must safeguard and account for all monies, documents, and other property received from a client or customer. State license laws regulate the broker's accounting obligations and escrow practices.

Full disclosure. An agent has the duty to inform the client of all material facts, reports, and rumors that might affect the client's interests in the property transaction.

Fiduciary Duties

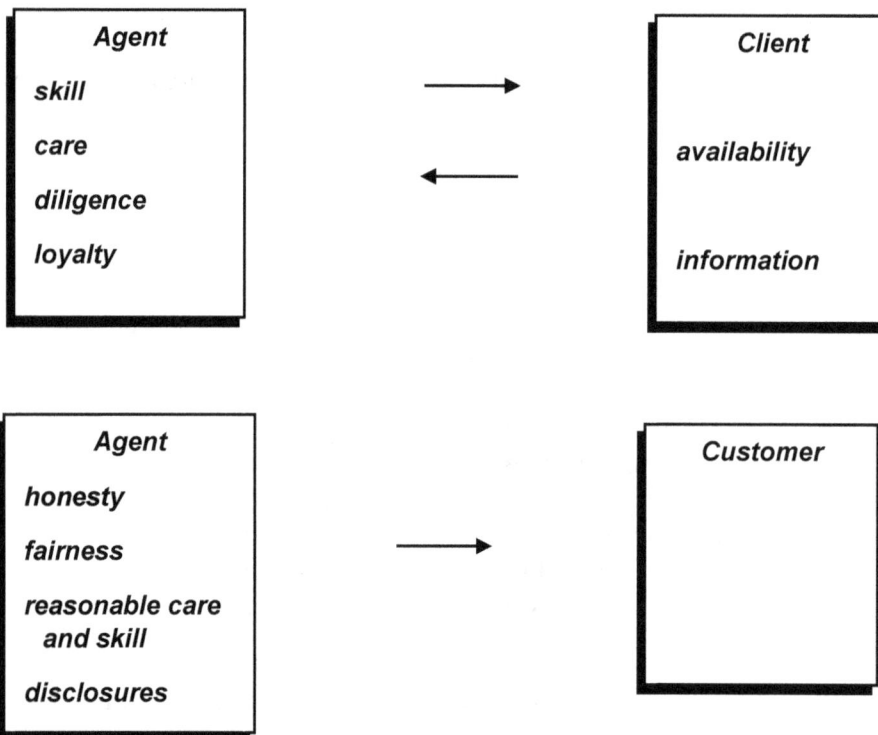

Agent		Client
skill	→	
care	←	*availability*
diligence		
loyalty		*information*

Agent		Customer
honesty		
fairness	→	
reasonable care and skill		
disclosures		

Full disclosure

An agent has the duty to inform the client of all material facts, reports, and rumors that might affect the client's interests in the property transaction.

In recent years, the disclosure standard has been raised to require an agent to disclose items that a practicing agent should know, whether the agent actually had the knowledge or not, and regardless of whether the disclosure furthers or impedes the progress of the transaction.

The most obvious example of a "should have known" disclosure is a property defect, such as an inoperative central air conditioner, that the agent failed to notice. If the air conditioner becomes a problem, the agent may be held liable for failing to disclose a material fact if a court rules that the typical agent in that area would detect and recognize a faulty air conditioner.

There is no obligation to obtain or disclose information related to a customer's race, creed, color, religion, sex or national origin: anti-discrimination laws hold such information to be immaterial to the transaction.

Some states have recently enacted laws requiring a seller to make a written disclosure about property condition to a prospective buyer. This seller disclosure may or may not relieve the agent of some liabilities for disclosure.

Disclosure of Material Facts

Critical material facts for disclosure include:

- the agent's opinion of the property's condition

- information about the buyer's motivations and financial qualifications

- discussions between agent and buyer regarding the possibility of the agent's representing the buyer in another transaction.

- adverse material facts, including property condition, title defects, environmental hazards, and property defects

Agent's duties to the customer

The traditional notion of caveat emptor-- let the buyer beware-- no longer applies unequivocally to real estate transactions. Agents do have certain obligations to customers, even though they do not represent them. In general, they owe a third party:

- honesty and fair dealing
- reasonable care and skill
- proper disclosure

Honesty. An agent has a duty to deal fairly and honestly with a customer. Thus, an agent may not deceive, defraud, or otherwise take advantage of a customer.

Reasonable care and skill. Reasonable skill and care" means that an agent will be held to the standards of knowledge, expertise, and ethics that are commonly maintained by other agents in the area.

Proper disclosure. Proper disclosure primarily concerns disclosure of agency, property condition, and environmental hazards.

An agent who fails to live up to prevailing standards may be held liable for negligence, fraud, or violation of state real estate license laws and regulations. Agents should be particularly careful about misrepresenting and offering inappropriate expert advice when working with customers.

Misrepresentation

Intentional misrepresentation. An agent may intentionally or unintentionally defraud a buyer by misrepresenting or concealing facts. While it is acceptable to promote the features of a property to a buyer or the virtues of a buyer to a seller, it is a fine line that divides promotion from misrepresentation. Silent misrepresentation, which is intentionally failing to reveal a material fact, is just as fraudulent as a false statement.

Negligent misrepresentation. An agent can be held liable for failure to disclose facts the agent was not aware of if it can be demonstrated that the agent should have known such facts. For example, if it is a common standard that agents inspect property, then an agent can be held liable for failing to disclose a leaky roof that was not inspected.

Misrepresentation of expertise. An agent should not act or speak outside the agent's area of expertise. A customer may rely on anything an agent says, and the agent will be held accountable. For example, an agent represents that a property will appreciate. The buyer interprets this as expert investment advice and buys the property. If the property does not appreciate, the buyer may hold the agent liable.

Principal's duties

The obligations of a principal in an agency relationship concern the following:

Availability. In a special agency, the power and decision-making authority of the agent are limited. Therefore, the principal must be available for consultation, direction, and decision-making. Otherwise, the agent cannot complete the job.

Information. The principal must provide the agent with a sufficient amount of information to complete the desired activity. This may include property data, financial data, and the client's timing requirements.

Compensation. If an agreement includes a provision for compensating the agent and the agent performs in accordance with the agreement, the client is obligated to compensate the agent. As indicated earlier, however, the agency relationship does not necessarily include compensation.

Breach of duty by agent

An agent is liable for a breach of duty to client or customer. Since clients and customers rely on the expertise and actions of agents performing within the scope of their authority, regulatory agencies and courts aggressively enforce agency laws, standards, and regulations.

A breach of duty may result in:

- rescission of the listing agreement (causing a loss of a potential commission)
- forfeiture of any compensation that may have already been earned
- disciplinary action by state license law authorities, including license suspension or revocation

SNAPSHOT REVIEW:

Unit 9: FIDUCIARY DUTIES

FIDUCIARY DUTIES

- agency relationship imposes fiduciary duties on client and agent

Agent's duties to the client

- **Skill, care, and diligence.** Agent to do job with diligence and competence

- **Loyalty.** Agent to place interest of client above others

- **Obedience.** Agent to comply with client directions

- **Confidentiality.** Agents hold in confidence client's personal or business information

- **Accounting.** Agent must safeguard and account for monies, documents, etc

- **Full disclosure.** Agent to inform client of material facts, reports, rumors

Full disclosure

- agent inform client of material facts, reports, rumors

- includes items agent "should have known"- broken AC, etc.

- some states require seller to provide written disclosure about property condition

Agent's duties to the customer

- **Honesty.** Agent to deal fairly and honestly

- **Reasonable care and skill.** Agent held to standards of knowledge, expertise, ethics maintained by other agents

- **Proper disclosure.** Agency, property condition, environmental hazards

Misrepresentation

- **Intentional misrepresentation.** Agent may intentionally/unintentionally defraud buyer if misrepresenting or concealing facts

- **Negligent misrepresentation.** Agent can be held liable for failure to disclose facts agent should have known

- **Misrepresentation of expertise.** Agent should not act outside area of expertise nor represent that they have expertise in areas where they do not

Principal's duties

- **Availability.** Principal available for consultation, direction, decision-making

- **Information.** Principal to provide agent with sufficient information to complete desired activity

- **Compensation.** Client obligated to compensate agent if agreement includes such provision

Breach of duty by agent

- may result in rescission of listing agreement; forfeiture of compensation; disciplinary action by state license law authorities

==

Check Your Understanding Quiz:

Unit 9: Fiduciary Duties

Carefully read each question and provide your best answer based on what you learned in this module. Then check your answers against the Answer Key which immediately follows the quiz questions.

1. Danny states without equivocation that a property will appreciate. What can he be accused of?

   a. Intentional misrepresentation
   b. Misrepresentation of expertise
   c. Negligent misrepresentation
   d. Fraud

2. Which of the following is an agent's duty to the customer?

   a. Proper disclosure
   b. Availability
   c. Loyalty
   d. Diligence

3. Which duty requires the agent to place the interests of the client above the agent's own?

   a. Obedience
   b. Confidentiality
   c. Loyalty
   d. Accounting

4. Proper disclosure primarily concerns agency, property condition and _____.

   a. compensation.
   b. crimes.
   c. demographics.
   d. environmental hazards.

5. Which duty requires an agent to uphold the standards maintained by other agents in the area?

   a. Reasonable care and skill
   b. Conformity
   c. Representation
   d. Honesty

==

Exercise Workshop -- Unit 9: Fiduciary Duties

Exercise 9-1. Fiduciary Duties

Synopsis:

In this exercise, the student will demonstrate their understanding of the difference between the duties owed to customers and clients.

Instructions:

1. Read the following statements and place the appropriate letter next to the statements if the duty is owed to a customer, client, or both.
2. Check your answers below.

Exercise:

    A. Client
    B. Customer
    C. Both
    D. Neither

_____ 1. Skill, care, and diligence

_____ 2. Loyalty

_____ 3. Obedience

_____ 4. Confidentiality

_____ 5. Account for all funds

_____ 6. Honesty

_____ 7. Fairness

_____ 8. Full disclosure

_____ 9. Reasonable care and skill

____ 10. Limited disclosure

Unit 10: Trust Fund Handling

Unit 10: Trust Fund Handling – Learning Objectives

When the student has completed Unit 10, he or she will be able to:

1. Describe the foundations of ethical practices in the context of managing the trust funds of third parties, with particular respect to timely depositing; account reconciliation; proper disbursement; commingling; and conversion

TRUST FUND HANDLING

The basic requirements of managing a South Carolina trust account are to

- include all information required by the South Carolina Real Estate Law
- identify the exact amount in the account at all times
- identify ownership of funds in the account, by amount, at all times
- provide a consistent and logical record of the account

Commingling and conversion

Commingling. Commingling means mixing or mingling operating funds with trust funds; for example, to deposit business account trust funds in the licensee's personal or general business account. Commingling is a strictly prohibited practice when dealing with escrow funds held in trust for others.

Conversion. Conversion means using trust funds for a purpose other than the purpose for which they are held. For example, a broker withdraws a sum of money from her trust account to pay the monthly rent – an operating expense that must come out of operating funds.

Conversion is a breach of trust and is a crime as provided by law.

TRUST ACCOUNT RULES

Broker-in-charge must manage. According to Section 40-57-136, when receiving funds belonging to another in connection with a real estate transaction, a broker-in-charge or property manager-in-charge must establish and maintain control of and responsibility for an active real estate trust account. This account must be a demand deposit account located in an insured financial institution authorized to conduct business in South Carolina.

The account must be designated and titled to include the word "*trust*" or the word "*escrow*" in the name of the respective broker-in-charge's firm or property manager-in-charge's real estate firm.

However, one central trust account may be used by real estate brokerage firms with multiple offices managed by one broker-in-charge or one property manager-in-charge and separate brokers-in-charge or separate property managers-in-charge.

The broker-in-charge or property manager-in-charge must educate employees and supervised licensees on the proper handling of trust funds.

A check or statement issued in connection with a real estate trust account must reflect the title and designation of the account as mentioned above.

Must maintain records. A broker-in-charge or property manager-in-charge must maintain records which reflect the transactions in that licensee's office and ensure that those records are accurate and complete. The licensee must also maintain backup copies for computerized real estate trust accounts on a data storage medium that is kept in a separate offsite location.

A broker-in-charge or property manager-in-charge **may not commingle trust funds of the client with his or her own money.** However, the licensee may maintain a clearly identified amount of the company's funds in the trust account to cover bank service charges or to avoid the closing of the account when no client's trust funds are on deposit.

Receipt and deposit of trust monies

Transmitting trust funds. Trust funds received by a supervised licensee in connection with a real estate transaction in which that licensee is engaged must be delivered to the supervising broker **no later than the following business day.**

Depositing funds. A broker-in-charge or property manager-in-charge who receives funds in a rental or lease transaction must deposit those funds in a real estate trust account as follows:

- cash or certified funds must be deposited within forty-eight hours of receipt, excluding Saturday, Sunday, and bank holidays
- checks must be deposited within forty-eight hours after a lease or rental agreement is signed by the parties to the transaction, excluding Saturday, Sunday, and bank holidays

A licensee who is directly employed by the owner of rental property may deposit rent in an operating or other similar account, but the licensee must properly account for the deposit. Note that an advance rental deposit is a trust fund and the licensee must treat it as such.

Retaining rental deposits. Trust funds received and deposited into the trust account in connection with a real estate rental or lease must remain in the trust account until the lease or rental transaction expires or is terminated. This includes, but is not limited to, security deposits, pet deposits, damage deposits, and advance rentals. When the lease expires or terminates, undisputed trust funds must be disbursed according to the terms of the contract. The licensee must also make a full accounting to the landlord or tenant.

The landlord must receive any earned rental proceeds within a reasonable time after clearance of the deposit by the bank.

Depositing deadlines. A broker-in-charge who receives funds in a real estate sales or exchange transaction must deposit the funds in a separate real estate trust account as follows:

- cash or certified funds must be deposited within *forty-eight hours of receipt*, excluding Saturday, Sunday, and bank holidays
- checks must be deposited within *forty-eight hours after written acceptance* of an offer by the parties to the transaction, excluding Saturday, Sunday, and bank holidays

Trust funds received in a real estate sales or exchange transaction and deposited in the trust account must remain in the trust account until consummation or termination of the transaction. When the transaction is consummated or terminated, the broker-in-charge holding the funds must disburse undisputed trust funds according to the terms of the contract. The licensee must also make a full accounting to the parties.

Interest-bearing accounts.

Trust funds received by a broker in charge or property manager in charge may be deposited in an interest-bearing account. The broker-in-charge or property manager-in-charge may keep the interest earned on these trust funds if both of the following are true:

- the depositors or owners of the trust funds have been informed of their right to ownership of the interest but give up the right of ownership to the broker-in-charge or property manager-in-charge by written agreement
- the agreement, if part of a preprinted form, uses conspicuous language

Trust fund disbursements

A broker-in-charge or property manager-in-charge who disburses trust funds from a designated trust account has properly fulfilled the duty to the account if the licensee disburses the funds under one of these circumstances:

- upon rejection of an offer to buy, sell, rent, lease, exchange, or option real estate
- upon the withdrawal of an offer not yet accepted by the offeree
- at the closing of the transaction

A broker-in-charge or property manager-in-charge who disburses trust funds contrary to the terms of the contract or fails to disburse trust funds not in dispute has demonstrated incompetence to act as a broker-in-charge or property manager-in-charge.

Money disputes. If a dispute arises between buyer and seller concerning the entitlement to and disposition of trust funds, and the dispute is not resolved reasonably by the parties, the deposit must be held in the trust account until the dispute is resolved by one of these means:

- a written agreement which directs the disposition of monies and is signed by all parties claiming an interest in the trust monies. The agreement must be separate from the contract which directs the broker-in-charge or property manager-in-charge to hold the monies.
- filing of an interpleader action in court. By filing such an action, the escrow agent may deposit the earnest money with the court according to the rules and procedures governing interpleader actions.
- order of a court
- voluntary mediation

Trust account recordkeeping

All trust accounts maintained by brokers-in-charge or property managers-in-charge must be located in an insured financial institution in South Carolina.

When required to establish and maintain a real estate trust account, the broker-in-charge or property manager-in-charge must also maintain a recordkeeping system in the licensee's designated principal place of business. The system should contain the following components:

- a journal or an accounting system that records the chronological sequence in which funds are received and disbursed for real estate sales. For funds received, the journal or accounting system must include the following information:
  o date of receipt
  o name of the party from whom the money was received
  o name of the principal
  o identification of the property
  o date of deposit
  o the depository
  o payee
  o check numbers, dates, and amounts

  The accounting system must keep a running balance for each entry of a receipt or disbursement. The journal or accounting system must provide a means of reconciling the accounts.

- a separate record for each tenant identifying the unit, the unit owner, amount of rent, due date, security deposit, and all receipts with dates when managing property.
  o The broker-in-charge or property manager-in-charge must also maintain an owner's ledger for all properties owned by each owner showing receipts and disbursements applicable to each property managed.
  o All disbursements must be documented by bids, contracts, invoices, or other appropriate written memoranda.
- a trust account deposit document identifying the buyer or tenant unless other appropriate written memoranda are maintained
- a general ledger identifying security deposits
- a monthly reconciliation of each separate account except when no deposit or disbursement was made during that month. The reconciliation must include a written worksheet comparing the reconciled bank balance with the journal balance and with the ledger total to ensure agreement.

Record retention. Trust fund records must be maintained for a minimum of five (5) years and the broker-in-charge or property manager-in-charge must furnish a copy of the records to a representative of the Commission upon request.

Accounting records that may be requested include, but are not limited to, journals, ledgers, folios, client subaccounts, tenant accounts, canceled checks, deposit slips, and bank statements.

SNAPSHOT REVIEW:

Unit 10: TRUST FUND HANDLING

TRUST FUND HANDLING

- include information required by SC real estate law; identify exact amount in account; who owns

- provide consistent and logical record

Commingling and conversion

- **Commingling.** Mixing or mingling personal and business funds

- **Conversion.** Using trust funds for purpose other than they are held for

TRUST ACCOUNT RULES

- **Broker-in-charge must manage.** Broker-in-charge maintains control of trust account

- **Must maintain records.** Records reflecting transactions in office; backup copies in off-site location

Receipt and deposit of trust monies

- **Transmitting trust funds.** Trust funds delivered to supervising broker by following business day

- **Depositing funds.** Rental or lease transaction funds to be deposited in trust account

- **Retaining rental deposits.** Rental/lease related funds to remain in trust account until lease/rental transaction expires or is terminated

- **Depositing deadlines.** Cash/certified funds deposited within 48 hours of receipt; checks deposited within 48 hours of written acceptance of offer

Trust fund disbursements

- **Money disputes.** Deposit held in trust account until dispute resolved by written agreement or filing of interpleader action in court

Trust account recordkeeping

- all trust accounts must be located in insured financial institution in SC

- **Record retention.** Trust fund records maintained for 5 years; broker-in-charge furnish copy to representative of Commission upon request

Check Your Understanding Quiz:

Unit 10: Trust Fund Handling

Carefully read each question and provide your best answer based on what you learned in this module. Then check your answers against the Answer Key which immediately follows the quiz questions.

1. If Mason uses trust funds to pay his rent, what can he be accused of?

    a. Commingling
    b. Mixing funds
    c. Conversion
    d. Borrowing

2. Security deposits for a rental must remain in the trust account until _____.

    a. the lease expires or is terminated.
    b. 30 days after the lease is signed.
    c. 60 days before the lease expires.
    d. 7 years have passed.

3. Trust fund records must be maintained for a minimum of _____.

    a. 6 months.
    b. 7 years.
    c. 12 months.
    d. 5 years.

4. If a broker-in-charge receives a trust fund deposit in cash, it must be deposited within _____.

    a. 24 hours of offer acceptance.
    b. 48 hours of receipt.
    c. 3 days of receipt.
    d. 5 days of offer acceptance.

===

Unit 11: Regulatory Compliance

Unit 11: Regulatory Compliance – Learning Objectives

When the student has completed Unit 11, he or she will be able to:

1. identify the foundations of competent practice as it is determined by compliance with brokerage practice laws and regulations

---

LICENSE LAW VIOLATIONS

One of the primary foundations of ethical and professional practices is executing the many tasks and duties of residential brokerage in compliance with the law. In turn, it is imperative to know and understand where these boundaries are and what actions are in fact violations of both ethical practice and the law. The following is a review of license law violations as set forth by statutes and regulations of South Carolina. Following this presentation is a summary of South Carolina's disciplinary process and just what penalties result when licensees fail to meet their professional standards of conduct.

According to Section 40-57-710, the Commission may deny a license to an applicant or may take disciplinary action against a licensee who performs any of the following actions:

1. makes a substantial misrepresentation on a real estate license application

2. makes a substantial misrepresentation involving a real estate transaction

3. makes false promises that are likely to influence, persuade, or induce

4. pursues a continued and deliberate course of misrepresentation or makes false and misleading promises through supervised licensees or through any form of advertising

5. demonstrates bad faith, dishonesty, untrustworthiness, or incompetency in a way that endangers the public interest

6. represents a real estate broker other than the employing broker-in-charge or property manager-in-charge

7. guarantees future profits from the resale of real estate

8. makes a dual set of contracts by stating a sales price other than the actual sales price

9. is convicted of violating the federal and state fair housing laws, forgery, embezzlement, breach of trust, larceny, obtaining money or property under false pretense, extortion, fraud, conspiracy to defraud in any state or federal court

10. has been convicted of a felony that is sex-related, drug-related, real estate-related, or is a financial or violent offense felony in any state or federal court

11. has pled guilty or nolo contendere to any of the above listed offenses in any state or federal court

12. fails to report to the Department in writing by certified mail, within ten (10) days, notice of conviction of any crime described above

13. fails, within a reasonable time, to account for or to remit trust funds which belong to others

14. pays compensation to an unlicensed individual for activities requiring a license. A licensee may not pay or offer to pay a referral or finder's fee to an unlicensed individual that is not a party in the real estate transaction.

15. violates any provision of law relating to the freedom of a buyer or seller to choose an attorney, insurance agent, title insurance agent, or any other service provider to facilitate the real estate transaction

16. fails to disclose the party or parties for whom the licensee will be acting as an agent in the real estate transaction

17. receives compensation from more than one party except with the full knowledge and written disclosure to all parties

18. represents more than one party in a transaction without the full written knowledge and consent of all parties

19. acts as an undisclosed principal

20. accepts deposit money which is to be delivered to the licensee's principal without informing the payor and having the payor acknowledge in writing who will hold the money the licensee received

21. issues a check in connection with the real estate business which is returned for insufficient funds or closed account

22. fails to disclose any known material fact concerning a real estate transaction

23. violates any provision Chapter 57 or a regulation promulgated under Chapter 57

24. violates a rule or order of the Commission

25. knowingly gives false information to an investigator or inspector

26. engages in a practice or takes action inconsistent with the agency relationship that other real estate licensees have established with their clients

27. fails to make all required records available to the Commission for inspection and copying upon a Commission investigator's request

28. fails to appear for an interview with a Commission investigator without due cause

29. provides false information to a direct inquiry by an investigator

30. fails to submit promptly all offers and counteroffers

31. fails to provide current contact information to the Commission

32. allows or creates an unreasonable delay in the closing or acts in a way that causes failure or termination of the transaction due solely to a dispute over the commission split

33. engages in wholesaling

LETTER OF CAUTION

A letter of caution may be issued for minor misconduct that does not require disciplinary action. It is a warning and not a form of discipline, unless explicitly stated. Letters of caution may be considered at future disciplinary hearings.

ARTIFICIAL INTELLIGENCE

Violations committed through the use of AI, machine learning, or similar programs are solely the responsibility of the licensee. These violations will be treated as if they were committed directly by the licensee.

THE DISCIPLINARY PROCESS

Investigations

If the Director of the Department of Labor, Licensing and Regulation has reason to believe that a licensee has violated the license law or has become unfit to practice real estate, the director may initiate an investigation. The director may also initiate an investigation if a person files a written complaint charging a licensee with a violation. Copies of these materials will be sent to the licensee's broker-in-charge who will be required to attend any disciplinary hearings if the behavior in question occurred during the broker-in-charge's supervision.

The investigation must be performed by investigators who have completed one hundred (100) hours of training in programs that are approved by the Commission and provide instruction on real estate principles, state statutory and regulatory law, and investigative techniques.

If the Commission believes the licensee is violating or intends to violate the license law, the Commission can order the licensee to "cease and desist" from the behavior. If the person being investigated is unlicensed, the Commission can apply to an administrative law judge for a temporary restraining order.

In conducting the investigation, the director may

- subpoena witnesses and compel their attendance

- take evidence
- require the production of anything that is relevant to the investigation including, but not limited to, the
    - existence, description, nature, custody, condition, and location of books, documents, or other tangible items
    - identity and location of persons having knowledge of relevant facts or anything else reasonably calculated to lead to the discovery of material evidence

If a person fails to obey a subpoena or to answer the director's questions, the director may apply to an administrative law judge for an order requiring the person to comply.

The department must complete its investigation within one hundred fifty (150) days of receiving the complaint or get a waiver from the Commission after showing due diligence and extenuating circumstances.

The Commission will designate the time and place of the hearing on the charges. The hearing must be conducted in accordance with the Administrative Procedures Act.

The Commission will render and serve the decision in writing to the charged licensee within ninety (90) days. The Commission must state the effective date of the ruling in the decision notice.

The department will post a report annually that provides the data for the:

- number of complaints received
- number of investigations initiated
- average length of investigations
- number of investigations that exceeded one hundred fifty days

Penalties

The commission may impose disciplinary action as follows:

- issue a public reprimand
- impose a fine up to ten thousand ($10,000) dollars for each violation. The commission may also recover the costs of the investigation and the prosecution.
- place a licensee on probation for a definite or indefinite time
- restrict or suspend the individual's license for a definite or indefinite time
- prescribe conditions to be met during probation, restriction, or suspension including, but not limited to, satisfactory completion of additional education, of a supervisory period, or of continuing education programs
- permanently revoke the license

A licensee may voluntarily enter into a consent order with the Commission in which the licensee does not contest the violations and accepts the sanctions. A licensee may also voluntarily surrender the license.

Appeals for administrative penalties may be filed within 10 days of receipt of the citation. Then the department will schedule a hearing before the Commission. If no appeal is filed, the penalties are due within 30 days of receipt of the citation.

SNAPSHOT REVIEW:

Unit 11: REGULATORY COMPLIANCE

LICENSE LAW VIOLATIONS

- misrepresentation; false promises; bad faith, dishonesty; guaranteeing future profits; freedom to choose vendor, etc.

- violating federal and state fair housing laws, forgery, embezzlement, breach of trust, larceny, obtaining money/property under false pretense, extortion, fraud, conspiracy to defraud in any state or federal court

- sex-related, drug-related, real-estate related felony

- paying unlicensed individual for activities requiring license

- a letter of caution may be issued as a warning for minor misconduct

- AI-assisted violations are treated as if they were committed directly by licensee

THE DISCIPLINARY PROCESS

Investigation procedures

- subpoena witnesses; take evidence; require production of relevant information

Penalties

- public reprimand

- fine up to $10,000 per violation

- probation

- restriction/suspension/revocation of license

===

Check Your Understanding Quiz:

Unit 11: Regulatory Compliance

Carefully read each question and provide your best answer based on what you learned in this module. Then check your answers against the Answer Key which immediately follows the quiz questions.

1. Who may initiate an investigation if there is reason to believe a licensee violated license law?

   a. The agent's broker
   b. Director of the Department of Labor, Licensing and Regulation
   c. Director of the local board of real estate
   d. NAR Director of Compliance

2. What is the maximum fine that the Commission is authorized to impose for a license law violation?

   a. $100,000
   b. $7,000
   c. $10,000
   d. $250

3. If the licensee fails to obey a subpoena, the director may apply to _____ for help.

   a. an administrative law judge
   b. the police
   c. a federal court judge
   d. the Supreme Court

4. Which of the following could result in the denial of a license?

   a. Disclosing all material facts
   b. Misrepresentation on a real estate license application
   c. Sharing environmental hazards with the buyer
   d. Discussing the steps needed to take to prepare a listing

5. The Commission will render and serve the decision in writing to the charged licensee within

   _____.

   a. 180 days.
   b. 6 months.
   c. 90 days.
   d. 1 month.

===

==

Exercise Workshop -- Unit 11: Regulatory Compliance

Exercise 11-1. Regulatory Compliance

Synopsis:

In this exercise, the student will demonstrate their understanding of licensing law and the penalties issued when a licensee violates licensing law.

Instructions:

1. Read the following passages.
2. Decide which penalty the Real Estate Commission would most likely levy.
3. Each answer may be used more than once, and each situation may have more than one answer.

NOTE: The Real Estate Commission can take mitigating and aggregating circumstances into account when hearing cases. For this exercise, answer with the most reasonable answer.

Exercise:

Penalties:

    A. Fine up to $10,000
    B. Agent put on probation
    C. Suspension of license
    D. Revocation of license
    E. Reprimand
    F. Additional Education

_____ 1. A real estate broker has an escrow account to hold escrow deposits for her clients. She routinely takes money from the escrow account and pays her personal bills with it. When she is supposed to turn the money over for closing, she tells the title company to lower her commission by the amount of the escrow deposit.

_____ 2. Agent Robert was convicted of arson in an insurance fraud case. He served minimal jail time and then was put on probation for five years. He never reported the conviction to the real estate commission.

_____ 3. Agent Nancy just executed a contract and is given a check for the escrow deposit. She takes the check to her bank and deposits it into her checking account. She does not turn the funds over to her Broker until the day before closing.

_____ 4. Agent Mike listed a house for sale and placed the listing in the MLS system. The seller told him that the roof leaked when there was heavy rain and wind. Agent Mike showed the house to a young couple looking to find their first home. Mike did not disclose to them the leak in the roof. The couple entered into a contract to buy the house and did not discover the leak until after closing.

_____ 5. Jill, a broker, tells all of her agents to tell their clients that they must use a specific title company and mortgage broker for all of their transactions. She tells them that these are the only companies they should use. What is not disclosed to the clients is that Jill owns these other companies.

Unit 12: Professional Practices

Unit 12: Property Disclosure – Learning Objectives

When the student has completed Unit 12, he or she will be able to:

1. Explain the critical foundations of fair housing law and ADA compliance with particular respect to anti-discriminatory activities; advertising violations; South Carolina's protected classes; and equal access to public accommodations

2. Summarize the central purposes and thrusts of the Fair Credit Act; describe the prohibition of redlining

3. Summarize the illegal practices of blockbusting, collusion, and market allocation, and why such practices are illegal

4. Generally characterize the purpose, structure and overall thrusts of the Realtors' Code of Ethics, Pathways to Professionalism and their Commitment to Excellence program

5. Explain the purpose and general content of a brokerage's policy and procedure's manual as it relates to the broker's duty to supervise and train subordinates

---

FAIR HOUSING

Federal and state governments have enacted laws prohibiting discrimination in the national housing market. The aim of these **fair housing laws,** or **equal opportunity housing laws,** is to give all people in the country an equal opportunity to live wherever they wish, provided they can afford to do so, without impediments of discrimination in the purchase, sale, rental, or financing of property.

Fair Housing and Local Zoning.

The Fair Housing Act prohibits a broad range of practices that discriminate against individuals on the basis of race, color, religion, sex, national origin, familial status, and disability. The Act does not preempt local zoning laws. However, the Act applies to municipalities and other local government entities and prohibits them from making zoning or land use decisions or implementing land use policies that exclude or otherwise discriminate against protected persons, including individuals with disabilities.

Forms of illegal discrimination

The Fair Housing Act specifically prohibits such activities in residential brokerage and financing as the following.

Discriminatory misrepresentation. An agent may not conceal available properties, represent that they are not for sale or rent, or change the sale terms for the purpose of discrimination. For example, an agent may not inform a minority buyer that the seller has recently decided not to carry back second mortgage financing when in fact the owner has made no such decision.

Discriminatory advertising. An agent may not advertise residential properties in such a way as to restrict their availability to any prospective buyer or tenant.

Providing unequal services. An agent may not alter the nature or quality of brokerage services to any party based on race, color, sex, national origin, or religion. For example, if it is customary for an agent to show a customer the latest MLS publication, the agent may not refuse to show it to any party. Similarly, if it is customary to show qualified buyers prospective properties immediately, an agent may not alter that practice for purposes of discrimination.

Steering. Steering is the practice of directly or indirectly channeling customers toward or away from homes and neighborhoods. Broadly interpreted, steering occurs if an agent describes an area in a subjective way for the purpose of encouraging or discouraging a buyer about the suitability of the area.

For example, an agent tells Buyer A that a neighborhood is extremely attractive, and that desirable families are moving in every week. The next day, the agent tells Buyer B that the same neighborhood is deteriorating, and that values are starting to fall. The agent has blatantly steered Buyer B away from the area and Buyer A into it.

Blockbusting. Blockbusting is the practice of inducing owners in an area to sell or rent to avoid an impending change in the ethnic or social makeup of the neighborhood that will cause values to go down.

For example, Agent Smith tells neighborhood owners that several minority families are moving in, and that they will be bringing their relatives next year. Smith informs homeowners that, in anticipation of a value decline, several families have already made plans to move.

Restricting MLS participation. It is discriminatory to restrict participation in any multiple listing service based on one's race, religion, national origin, color, or sex.

Redlining. Redlining is the residential financing practice of refusing to make loans on properties in a certain neighborhood regardless of a mortgagor's qualifications. In effect, the lender draws a red line around an area on the map and denies all financing to applicants within the encircled area.

AMERICANS WITH DISABILITIES ACT

Purpose. The ADA, which became law in 1990, is a civil rights law that prohibits discrimination against individuals with disabilities in all areas of public life, including employment, education, transportation, and facilities that are open to the general public. The purpose of the law is to make sure that people with disabilities have the same rights and opportunities as everyone else.

The Americans with Disabilities Act Amendments Act. The ADAAA became effective on January 1, 2009. Among other things, the ADAAA clarified that a disability is "a physical or mental impairment that substantially limits one or more major life activities." This definition applies to all titles of the ADA and covers private employers with 15 or more employees, state and local governments, employment agencies, labor unions, agents of the employer, joint management labor committees, and private entities considered places of public accommodation. Examples of the latter include hotels, restaurants, retail stores, doctor's offices, golf courses, private schools, day care centers, health clubs, sports stadiums, and movie theaters.

Components. The ADA / ADAAA consists of five parts.

1. Title I (**Employment**) concerns equal employment opportunity. It is enforced by the U.S. Equal Employment Opportunity Commission.
2. Title II (**State and Local government**) concerns nondiscrimination in state and local government services. It is enforced by the U.S. Department of Justice.
3. Title III (**Public Accommodations**) concerns nondiscrimination in public accommodations and commercial facilities. It is enforced by the U.S. Department of Justice.
4. Title IV (**Telecommunications**) concerns accommodations in telecommunications and public service messaging. It is enforced by the Federal Communications Commission.
5. Title V (**Miscellaneous**) concerns a variety of general situations including how the ADA affects other laws, insurance providers, and lawyers.

Real estate practitioners are most likely to encounter Titles I and III and should acquire familiarity with these. In advising clients, licensees are well-advised to seek qualified legal counsel.

Requirements. The ADA requires landlords in certain circumstances to modify housing and facilities so that disabled persons can access them without hindrance.

The ADA also requires that disabled employees and members of the public be provided access that is equivalent to that provided to those who are not disabled.

- Employers with at least fifteen employees must follow nondiscriminatory employment and hiring practices.
- Reasonable accommodations must be made to enable disabled employees to perform essential functions of their jobs.
- Modifications to the physical components of a building may be necessary to provide the required access to tenants and their customers, such as widening doorways, changing door hardware, changing how doors open, installing ramps, lowering wall-mounted telephones and keypads, supplying Braille signage, and providing auditory signals.
- Existing barriers must be removed when the removal is "readily achievable," that is, when cost is not prohibitive. New construction and remodeling must meet a higher standard.
- If a building or facility does not meet requirements, the landlord must determine whether restructuring or retrofitting or some other kind of accommodation is most practical.

Penalties. Violations of ADA requirements can result in citations, business license restrictions, fines, and injunctions requiring remediation of the offending conditions. Business owners may also be held liable for personal injury damages to an injured plaintiff.

FAIR FINANCING LAWS

Parallel anti-discrimination and consumer protection laws have been enacted in the mortgage financing field to promote equal opportunity in housing.

Equal Credit Opportunity Act (ECOA). Enacted in 1974, the Equal Credit Opportunity Act requires lenders to be fair and impartial in determining who qualifies for a loan. A lender may not discriminate on the basis of race, color, religion, national origin, sex, marital status, or age. The act also requires lenders to inform prospective borrowers who are being denied credit of the reasons for the denial.

Home Mortgage Disclosure Act. This statute requires lenders involved with federally guaranteed or insured loans to exercise impartiality and non-discrimination in the geographical distribution of their loan portfolio. In other words, the act is designed to prohibit redlining. It is enforced in part by requiring lenders to report to authorities where they have placed their loans.

Equal Opportunity in Housing Poster

U. S. Department of Housing and Urban Development

EQUAL HOUSING OPPORTUNITY

We Do Business in Accordance With the Federal Fair Housing Law

(The Fair Housing Amendments Act of 1988)

It is illegal to Discriminate Against Any Person Because of Race, Color, Religion, Sex, Handicap, Familial Status, or National Origin

- In the sale or rental of housing or residential lots
- In advertising the sale or rental of housing
- In the financing of housing
- In the provision of real estate brokerage services
- In the appraisal of housing
- Blockbusting is also illegal

Anyone who feels he or she has been discriminated against may file a complaint of housing discrimination:
1-800-669-9777 (Toll Free)
1-800-927-9275 (TTY)
www.hud.gov/fairhousing

U.S. Department of Housing and Urban Development
Assistant Secretary for Fair Housing and Equal Opportunity
Washington, D.C. 20410

Previous editions are obsolete

form HUD-928.1 (6-2011)

Anti-trust laws

Brokerage companies, like other businesses, are subject to anti-trust laws designed to prevent monopolies and unfair trade practices.

Sherman Antitrust Act. Enacted in 1890, the Sherman Antitrust Act prohibits restraint of interstate and foreign trade by conspiracy, monopolistic practice, and certain forms of business combinations, or mergers. The Sherman Act empowers the federal government to proceed against antitrust violators.

Clayton Antitrust Act. The Clayton Antitrust Act of 1914 reinforces and broadens the provisions of the Sherman Act. Among its prohibitions are certain exclusive contracts, predatory price cutting to eliminate competitors, and inter-related boards of directors and stock holdings between same-industry corporations. The Clayton Act also legalizes certain labor strikes, picketing, and boycotts.

Anti-competitive behavior. The effect of antitrust legislation is to prohibit trade practice and trade restraints that unfairly disadvantage open competition. Business practices and behaviors which violate antitrust laws include collusion, price fixing, market allocation, bid rigging, restricting market entry, exclusive dealing, and predatory pricing.

Collusion. Collusion is the illegal practice of two or more businesses joining forces or making joint decisions which have the effect of putting another business at a competitive disadvantage. Businesses may not collude to fix prices, allocate markets, create monopolies, or otherwise interfere with free market operations.

Price fixing. Price fixing is the practice of two or more brokers agreeing to charge certain commission rates or fees for their services, regardless of market conditions or competitors. In essence, such pricing avoids and disturbs the dynamics of a free, open market.

For instance, the two largest brokerages in a market jointly decide to cut commission rates by 50% in order to draw clients away from competitors. The cut-rate pricing could destroy smaller agencies that lack the staying power of the large companies.

Market allocation. Market allocation is the practice of colluding to restrict competitive activity in portions of a market in exchange for a reciprocal restriction from a competitor: "we won't compete against you here if you won't compete against us there."

For example, Broker A agrees to trade only in single family re-sales, provided that Broker B agrees to focus exclusively on apartment rentals and condominium sales. The net effect is an illegally restricted market where collusion and monopoly supplant market forces.

Tie-in agreements. In a tie-in agreement, the sale of one product or performance of a service is tied to the sale of another, less desirable product or service. For instance, "I will sell you this car, but you have to hire my brother-in-law to drive it." Or, more likely, "I will list and sell your old home if you hire me to find you a new home to purchase." Tie-ins restrict competition and limit the freedom of the consumer.

Violations of fair trade and anti-trust laws may be treated as felonies, and penalties can be substantial. Loss of one's license is also at stake. Brokers are well-advised to understand and recognize these laws.

CODES OF ETHICS

The real estate industry has developed a code of professional standards and ethics as a guideline in serving the real estate needs of consumers. This professional code has emerged from three primary sources:

- federal and state legislation
- state real estate licensing regulation
- industry self-regulation through trade associations and institutes

Federal legislation focuses primarily on anti-discrimination laws and fair-trade practices. State laws and licensing regulations focus on agency and disclosure requirements and regulating certain brokerage practices within the state jurisdiction. Real estate trade groups focus on professional standards of conduct in every facet of the business.

By observing professional ethics and standards, licensees will serve clients and customers better, foster a professional image in the community, and avoid regulatory sanctions and lawsuits.

Trade associations representing the real estate industry have instituted their own codes of ethics and professional practices covering every facet of brokerage activity. For the latest 2021 Code of Ethics of the National Association of REALTORS®, see

https://www.nar.realtor/about-nar/governing-documents/code-of-ethics/2024-code-of-ethics-standards-of-practice

NATIONAL ASSOCIATION OF REALTORS® CODE OF ETHICS

Historical abstract

In 1908, the National Association of Realtors® (NAR) formed to eliminate the notion of "Caveat emptor" or let the buyer beware. Their goal was to protect the public and promote homeownership in the United States.

In 1913, NAR introduced the Code of Ethics for Realtors® to follow in their dealings with their clients, the public, and other Realtors®. This document has been fluid and ever-changing over the years. Today, Realtors® have one of the strongest professional Code of Ethics in the United States.

The Code of Ethics also provides standard practices and procedures setting forth how Realtors® should react in their dealings with specific individuals and others in their field. The Code of Ethics, however, is not law. Rather, the Code of Ethics enhances local, state, or federal laws.

Structure of the Code of Ethics

The Code of Ethics has four parts:

- The Preamble

- Duties to Clients and Customers (Articles 1 – 9)

- Duties to the Public (Articles 10 – 14)

- Duties to Realtors® (Articles 15 – 17)

The Articles within the Code of Ethics define the broad statements about the licensee's behavior and duties. The Standards of Practice, within each Article, gives more specific guidance to the licensee. The Standards of Practice support and interpret the Articles.

The Preamble

The Preamble of the Code of Ethics serves as a vision statement on how licensees should conduct themselves and represent their profession to the public. The Preamble calls for Realtors® to "maintain and improve the standards of their calling." It also states that it is the Realtor's responsibility to "act with integrity and honesty."

SECTION 1 – DUTIES TO CLIENTS AND CUSTOMERS

SECTION 1: DUTIES TO CLIENTS AND CUSTOMERS

- **covers the first 9 Articles**
- **Standards of practices are more detailed requirements of each Article within the Code of Ethics.**

ARTICLE 1

- promotes honesty to all.

ARTICLE 2

- Realtor's® actions must have transparency to them.

ARTICLE 3

- promotes cooperation among brokers unless it is not in their client's best interest.

ARTICLE 4

- Realtors® must disclose that they have a real estate license when buying, selling, or renting their own property.

ARTICLE 5

- Realtors® must disclose any conflict of interest before providing professional services.

ARTICLE 6

- Realtors® may not accept any compensation without the written consent of all parties.

ARTICLE 7

- Realtors may not accept compensation from more than one person without disclosing the fact to all parties.

ARTICLE 8

- addresses the handling of escrow funds.

ARTICLE 9

- states that all documents must be in clear and concise language.

SECTION 2 – DUTIES TO THE PUBLIC

ARTICLE 10

- Realtors® must give equal professional service to all clients and customers irrespective of race, color, religion, sex, handicap, familial status, national origin, sexual orientation, or sexual identity
- Realtors do not discriminate in their employment practices

ARTICLE 11

- Realtors® must be knowledgeable and competent in their fields of practice
- If not competent, must get assistance from a knowledgeable professional or disclose any lack of experience to their client

ARTICLE 12

- Realtors® must be honest and truthful in their communications
- must present accurate descriptions in advertising, marketing, other public representations

ARTICLE 13

- Realtors® must not engage in the unauthorized practice of law

ARTICLE 14

- Realtors® must willingly participate in an ethics investigation and enforcement actions.

SECTION 3 –DUTIES TO REALTORS®

ARTICLE 15

- Realtors® must be truthful, make objective comments about other real estate professionals.

ARTICLE 16

- respect exclusive brokerage relationships of other Realtors® with their clients

ARTICLE 17

- arbitrate financial disagreements with other Realtors® and with their clients.

PATHWAYS TO PROFESSIONALISM

While the Code of Ethics establishes enforceable standards that Realtors® must follow, it does not set out standards of common courtesy or etiquette that a Realtors® should use in their dealings with other Realtors® or the public. This is accomplished with NAR's set of professional courtesy standards called the Pathways to Professionalism.

There are three sections to the Pathways to Professionalism:

1. Respect for the Public

2. Respect for Property

3. Respect for Peers

These Professional courtesies are intended to be used by REALTORS® voluntarily. Its specific provisions by section are as follows.

Pathways to Professionalism

Respect for the Public

1. Follow the "Golden Rule": Do unto others as you would have them do unto you.
2. Respond promptly to inquiries and requests for information.
3. Schedule appointments and showings as far in advance as possible.
4. Call if you are delayed or must cancel an appointment or showing.
5. If a prospective buyer decides not to view an occupied home, promptly explain the situation to the listing broker or the occupant.
6. Communicate with all parties in a timely fashion.
7. When entering a property, ensure that unexpected situations, such as pets, are handled appropriately.
8. Leave your business card if not prohibited by local rules.
9. Never criticize property in the presence of the occupant.
10. Inform occupants that you are leaving after showings.
11. When showing an occupied home, always ring the doorbell or knock—and announce yourself loudly before entering. Knock and announce yourself loudly before entering any closed room.
12. Present a professional appearance at all times; dress appropriately and drive a clean car.
13. If occupants are home during showings, ask their permission before using the telephone or bathroom.
14. Encourage the clients of other brokers to direct questions to their agent or representative.
15. Communicate clearly; don't use jargon or slang that may not be readily understood.
16. Be aware of and respect cultural differences.
17. Show courtesy and respect to everyone.
18. Be aware of—and meet—all deadlines.
19. Promise what you can deliver—and keep your promises.
20. Identify your REALTOR® and your professional status in contacts with the public.

21. Do not tell people what you think—tell them what you know.

Respect for Property

1. Be responsible for everyone you allow to enter listed property.
2. Never allow buyers to enter listed property unaccompanied.
3. When showing property, keep all members of the group together.
4. Never allow unaccompanied access to the property without permission.
5. Enter property only with permission, even if you have a lockbox key or combination.
6. When the occupant is absent, please leave the property as you found it (lights, heating, cooling, drapes, etc.) If you think something is amiss (e.g., vandalism), contact the listing broker immediately.
7. Be considerate of the seller's property. Do not allow anyone to eat, drink, smoke, dispose of trash, use bathing or sleeping facilities, or bring pets. Leave the house as you found it unless instructed otherwise.
8. Use sidewalks; if weather is bad, take off shoes and boots inside the property.
9. Respect sellers' instructions about photographing or videographing their properties' interiors or exteriors.

Respect for Peers

1. Identify your REALTOR® and professional status in all contacts with other REALTORS®.
2. Respond to other agents' calls, faxes, and e-mails promptly and courteously.
3. Be aware that large electronic files with attachments or lengthy faxes may be a burden on recipients.
4. Notify the listing broker if there appears to be inaccurate information on the listing.
5. Share important information about a property, including pets, security systems, and whether sellers will be present during the showing.
6. Show courtesy, trust, and respect to other real estate professionals.
7. Avoid the inappropriate use of endearments or other denigrating language.
8. Do not prospect at other REALTORS®' open houses or similar events.
9. Return keys promptly.
10. Carefully replace keys in the lockbox after showings.
11. To be successful in the business, mutual respect is essential.
12. Real estate is a reputation business. What you do today may affect your reputation—and business—for years to come.

The above is from the 2021 NAR Code of Ethics and Arbitration Manual, Pathways to Professionalism, page vii. https://www.nar.realtor/code-of-ethics-and-arbitration-manual/pathways-to-professionalism

Commitment to Excellence (C2EX)

The Commitment to Excellence (C2EX) program from the National Association of REALTORS® is a professional development resource that empowers REALTORS® to evaluate, enhance and showcase their highest professional levels. It's not a course, class, or designation—it's an Endorsement that REALTORS® can promote when serving clients and other REALTORS®.

The NAR Board of Directors has requested that all Board of Directors, committee members, and leadership complete the C2EX program. To date, over 50,000 Realtors® have completed this program.

OTHER PROFESSIONAL PRACTICES

Ethical practices in real estate brokerage manifest themselves through the professional's fulfillment of fiduciary duties, competence in handling trust funds, complying with the body of South Carolina license laws, adhering to the tenets of fair housing, and abiding by the general ethos of the Realtors' Code of Ethics. Another way of understanding these standards is from the point of view of the licensee's job performance in the context of discharging one's duties. These can be summarized as follows.

Duties to clients

Most codes of ethics uphold the commitment to fulfill fiduciary duties. Specific applications include:

- honestly representing market value and property condition
- respecting rights and duties of other client-agent relationships
- submitting all offers
- avoiding commingling and conversion
- keeping transaction documents current
- maintaining confidentiality
- managing client property competently

Duties to customers

Some of the guidelines for working with customers are:

- honestly representing market value and property condition
- avoiding calling a service "free" that in fact is contingent on receiving a commission
- advertising truthfully

Disclosure

- In compliance with applicable laws and to promote respect for the real estate profession, licensees should be careful to disclose
- that the agent is going to receive compensation from more than one party in a transaction
- property defects if they are reasonably apparent; however there is no duty to disclose a defect which it would require technical expertise to discover
- any interest the agent has in a listed property if the agent is representing a party concerning the property
- any profits made on a client's money
- the agent's identity in advertisements
- the agent's representation of both parties in a transaction
- the existence of accepted offers
- identity of broker and firm in advertising as required by state law

SNAPSHOT REVIEW:

Unit 12: PROFESSIONAL PRACTICES

FAIR HOUSING

- provide equal opportunity to live anywhere without discrimination in purchase, sale, renting, financing

Fair Housing and Local Zoning

- prohibits discrimination based on race, color, religion, sex, national origin, familial status, disability

- does not pre-empt local zoning laws

- applies to municipalities, local government entities making zoning/land use decisions

Forms of illegal discrimination

- **Discriminatory misrepresentation.** Agent may not conceal available properties or change sale terms

- **Discriminatory advertising.** Agent may not restrict property availability in advertising properties

- **Providing unequal services.** Agent may not provide preferential service from one party to the next

- **Steering.** Directly/indirectly channeling customers toward/away from homes

- **Blockbusting.** Inducing owners to sell/rent to avoid purportedly adverse changes in ethnic makeup of neighborhood

- **Restricting MLS participation.** Restrict participation in MLS arbitrarily

- **Redlining.** Refusing to make loans on properties in certain neighborhoods

AMERICANS WITH DISABILITIES ACT

- **Purpose.** Civil rights law prohibiting discrimination against individuals with disabilities in public life, employment, education, transportation, public facilities

- **The Americans with Disabilities Act Amendments Act.** Disability is "physical or mental impairment that substantially limits one or more major life activities."

- **Focus areas.** Employment; state and local government; public accommodations; telecommunications; miscellaneous

- **Requirements.** Within reason, must modify housing/facilities for disabled person's access

- **Penalties.** Citations, business license restrictions, fines, injunctions requiring remediation of offending conditions, personal injury damages

FAIR FINANCINGS LAWS

- **Equal Credit Opportunity Act (ECOA).** Lenders must exercise fairness in qualifying loan applicants

- **Home Mortgage Disclosure Act.** Prohibits redlining for lenders

Anti-trust laws

- **Sherman Antitrust Act.** Prohibits restraint of interstate/foreign trade by conspiracy, monopolistic practice, business combinations, or mergers

- **Clayton Antitrust Act.** Reinforces/broadens antitrust provisions of Sherman Act

- **Anti-competitive behavior.** Prohibit trade practices that unfairly disadvantage competitor

- **Collusion.** Illegal practice of 2+ businesses joining forces to put another business at competitive disadvantage

- **Price fixing.** 2+ brokers agreeing to charge certain commission rates or fees for their services

- **Market allocation.** Colluding to restrict competitive activity in portions of market in exchange for reciprocal restriction from competitor; establishing restrictive territories

- **Tie-in agreements.** Sale of product or performance of service tied to sale of another, less desirable product or service

CODE OF ETHICS

- guideline for real estate needs of consumers

- sourced from federal and state legislation; state real estate licensing regulation; industry self-regulation through trade associations/institutes

NATIONAL ASSOCIATION OF REALTORS® CODE OF ETHICS

Historical abstract

- NAR formed to eliminate "Caveat emptor" and protect public and promote homeownership

- established standard practices/procedures how Realtors® should react in dealings with individuals and others in field

Structure of the Code of Ethics

The Preamble

- vision statement on how licensees should conduct themselves/represent profession to public

SECTION 1- DUTIES TO CLIENTS AND CUSTOMERS

- **Article 1.** Honesty to all

- **Article 2.** Transparency

- **Article 3.** Cooperation among brokers

- **Article 4.** Disclose license when buying, selling, renting

- **Article 5.** Disclose conflicts of interest

- **Article 6.** Written consent of all parties for compensation

- **Article 7.** May not accept compensation from more than 1 person without disclosing to all parties

- **Article 8.** Escrow fund handling

- **Article 9.** Clear and concise language

SECTION 2- DUTIES TO THE PUBLIC

- **Article 10.** Equal professional service to all clients

- **Article 11.** Knowledgeable and competent in fields of practice

- **Article 12.** Honesty in communications

- **Article 13.** Must not engage in unauthorized practice of law

- **Article 14.** Must participate in ethics investigation and enforcement actions

SECTION 3 –DUTIES TO REALTORS®

- **Article 15.** Truthful about other real estate professionals

- **Article 16.** Respect brokerage relationships

- **Article 17.** Arbitrate financial disagreements

PATHWAYS TO PROFESSIONALISM

- standards of common courtesy or etiquette Realtors® should use in dealings with other Realtors® or public

- respect for Public, Property, Peers

Respect for the Public

- do unto others as you would have them do unto you
- respect people's time
- professional appearance

- keep your promises

Respect for Property

- be responsible for everyone you allow into a home

- leave property as found

Respect for Peers

- respond to other agents promptly

- courtesy, trust, respect

- return keys promptly

Commitment to Excellence (C2EX)

- professional development resource empowering Realtors® to evaluate, enhance, showcase highest professional levels

OTHER PROFESSIONAL PRACTICES

Duties to clients

- commitment to fulfill fiduciary duties

- submitting all offers; avoiding commingling/conversion; confidentiality, etc.

Duties to customers

- honestly representing market value, condition; avoiding calling service free that is contingent on receiving commission; advertising truthfully

Disclosure

- disclose any interest agent has in listed property; any profits made on client's money; agent's identity in advertisements, etc.

===

Check Your Understanding Quiz:

Unit 12: Professional Practices

Carefully read each question and provide your best answer based on what you learned in this module. Then check your answers against the Answer Key which immediately follows the quiz questions.

1. Abigail reached out to a property manager about an apartment that was listed as available online. When the property manager found out she was female, he said it was no longer available. What can he be accused of?

    a. Redlining
    b. Discrimination
    c. Blockbusting
    d. Restricting MLS participation

2. Which statute prohibits discrimination against individuals with disabilities in employment?

    a. The Americans with Disabilities Act
    b. The Discrimination in Employment Act
    c. The Fair Housing Act
    d. The Disabilities Discrimination Act

3. Which statute prohibits lenders from discriminating on the basis of religion?

    a. Home Mortgage Disclosure Act
    b. Market Allocation Act
    c. Equal Credit Opportunity Act
    d. Regulation Z

4. What is the primary focus of Section 1 of the Code of Ethics?

    a. Duties to the public
    b. The Preamble
    c. Duties to Peers
    d. Duties to clients and customers

5. What is the name of the standards NAR established for Realtors® to use when dealing with each other?

    a. Realtors® Respect Statute
    b. Respect for the Public
    c. Pathways to Professionalism
    d. Co-broker Etiquette Standards

6. What is it called when an agent directly channels a customer away from a neighborhood?

   a. Steering
   b. Guiding
   c. Blockbusting
   d. Directing

7. Which statute prohibits monopolistic practice?

   a. Collusion Act
   b. Price Fixing Act
   c. Fair Housing Law
   d. Sherman Antitrust Act

8. Clay and Andrew are competitors, so they decide that they both will focus on two separate neighborhoods. Clay said he won't compete with him in the Heights as long as Andrew leaves the Pleasantville subdivision to Clay. What is this agreement called?

   a. Price fixing
   b. Market allocation
   c. Monopoly
   d. Tie-in agreement

9. What is the name of the professional development resource for Realtors® developed by NAR?

   a. Commitment to Ethics
   b. Etiquette Course
   c. Commitment to Excellence
   d. Platinum Ethics Designation

10. Which statute prohibits redlining?

    a. Home Mortgage Disclosure Act
    b. Redlining Prohibition Act
    c. Housing Discrimination Act
    d. ECOA

11. Various codes of ethics emerged in real estate practice from federal and state legislation, state real estate licensing regulation, and _____.

    a. NAR.
    b. industry self-regulation through trade associations and institutes.
    c. Fair Housing Laws.
    d. local jurisdictions.

12. What are the three sections to Pathways to Professionalism?

    a. Respect for Customers, Respect for Clients, and Respect for Agents
    b. Respect for Brokers, Respect for Lenders, and Respect for Peers
    c. Respect for the Law, Respect for Property, and Respect for Clients
    d. Respect for the Public, Respect for Property, and Respect for Peers

13. Anna tells her client that she will list and sell her old home if she hires her as a buyer's agent for her future home. What is the name of this agreement?

    a. Tie-in agreement
    b. Joint brokerage agreement
    c. Dual agent agreement
    d. Collusion agreement

14. Which statute prohibits predatory price cutting to eliminate competitors?

    a. Trust Violation Act
    b. Price Fixing Act
    c. Clayton Antitrust Act
    d. Monopoly Act

15. What is the name of the practice of inducing owners to sell their homes in order to avoid financial losses resulting from an impending change in the ethnic makeup of the neighborhood?

    a. Steering
    b. Blockbusting
    c. Redlining
    d. Price gouging

===

Exercise Workshop -- Unit 12: Professional Practices

Exercise 12-1. Anti-Discrimination and Fair Housing

Synopsis:

In this exercise, the student will evaluate a scenario and determine which law was violated and what caused the violation.

Instructions:

1. Read each passage carefully.
2. State the law violated.
3. How the law was violated.
4. Compare your answers to the explanations given in the Answers section of this exercise.

Exercise:

1. Broker Barbara has a client who is Vietnamese. The client is looking to buy a new home and tells Barbara that she wants to buy in a neighborhood that has other Asian people in it. Barbara takes her to a specific community that is known as Little Vietnam.

2. John is trying to get a loan to buy a piece of property that the city council is selling. The property is in a poorer section of town with a high crime rate. The bank refuses to give John a loan because of the property's location, even though John meets all of the requirements to get the loan.

3. Shelly is a wheelchair user and is looking to rent a new apartment. She finds an apartment she likes but needs to have several railings added to it. When she talks with the landlord about renting the unit, he states that he does not have to make the changes because it would cost too much money and that because of the damage the chair will do to his unit, he is going to increase her rent and charge her a high deposit than stated in his ad.

4. The brokers of three major brokerages in town get together to have lunch. They begin talking about ways they can make more money. They decide amongst themselves to increase their commission percentage to 7% on all new listings.

5. Agent Jeanie has listed a house for a couple. She finds a buyer for the house and brings an offer to the sellers. They ask her if the buyer is white. She tells them no, that the buyer is black. The couple states that they will not sell to a black person. Jeanie cautions that it is illegal to refuse to sell to someone because of their color, and that fair housing enforcement has recently been on the rise in the area. The seller agrees to accept the offer.

Exercise Workshop – Unit 12: Professional Practice

Exercise 12-2. Realtor's Code of Ethics

Synopsis:

In this exercise, the student will demonstrate their understanding of NAR's Realtor's® Code of Ethics and their duties to their customers, clients, and other Realtors®.

Instructions:

Answer the following questions with an outright answer or by citing which portion of the Code of Ethics is applicable to the solution.

Exercise:

1. The _____ states that real estate agents should use the "Golden Rule" in their dealings with the public.

2. The Pathways to Professionalism defines the standards of common courtesy that a Realtor® should use in dealing with _____.

3. The National Association of Realtors® implemented the Code of Ethics in _____.

4. _____ is a new program created by NAR that empowers Realtors® to evaluate, enhance, and showcase their highest professional levels.

5. The Preamble of the Code of Ethics states that it is a Realtor's® responsibility to
    _____.

6. Broker Alice has a friend who bought a home from another agent. Her friend did not have a good experience with his agent. Alice suggested that he set up a meeting with his agent's Broker. He sets up an appointment and asks Alice to go with him to the meeting.

    At the meeting, he introduces Alice as a friend and adviser. Alice sits through the meeting and does not announce that she is a real estate agent. Later, when the Broker learns that Alice was a licensed broker and did not reveal that fact, she brings her up on Ethics charges. Which part of the Code of Ethics was Alice guilty of violating?

7. Which Article did NAR change in 2020 to include all of a Realtors® action, not just activities in a real estate transaction? This was done to protect the public trust in the Realtor® name.

Module D: MEASUREMENT AND VALUATION

Unit 13: Measuring Real Property
Unit 14: Real Property Valuation

Module D Learning Objectives

Measuring Real Property

1. Define and characterize the principal forms of legal descriptions, (metes and bounds and Rectangular Survey) and how they work

2. Calculate the acreage of a section or fractional portion thereof

3. Derive the area of a given parcel of real estate given its perimeter lengths

4. Describe the considerations involved in deriving a dwelling's living area given its general features and dimensions

5. Define and differentiate the commercial property concepts of rentable versus usable area; load factors and efficiency factors

Real Property Valuation

1. Describe how the economic principles of supply and demand impact real property values and real estate market cycles

2. Identify the key differentiations between an appraisal and a broker's opinion of value

3. Summarize the valuation principles of substitution, contribution, depreciation and obsolescence

4. Describe the process of completing a Comparative Market Analysis and summarize the uses of the value estimate it derives

5. Summarize how to adjust comparables given differences between the comp and the subject; summarize how to reconcile all the CMA's adjustments

Unit 13: Measuring Real Property

When the student has completed Unit 13, he or she will be able to:

1. Define and characterize the principal forms of legal descriptions, (metes and bounds and Rectangular Survey) and how they work

2. Calculate the acreage of a section or fractional portion thereof

3. Derive the area of a given parcel of real estate given its perimeter lengths

4. Describe the considerations involved in deriving a dwelling's living area given its general features and dimensions

In this unit, we will examine the various ways real property is described and measured. The principal measures examined include describing and measuring large tracts of land (legal descriptions, townships, acreage); measuring smaller units of land area (lots, foot frontages); and measuring real property improvements, including both residential and commercial forms of measurement (living area and rentable/usable area).

METHODS OF LEGAL DESCRIPTION

A legal description of real property is one which *accurately locates and identifies the boundaries of the subject parcel to a degree acceptable by courts of law in the state where the property is located.*

The general criterion for a legal description is that it alone provides sufficient data for a surveyor to locate the parcel. A legal description identifies the property as unique and distinct from all other properties.

Legal description provides accuracy and consistency over time. Systems of legal description, in theory, facilitate transfers of ownership and prevent boundary disputes and problems with chain of title.

A legal description is required for:
public recording
- creating a valid deed of conveyance or lease
- completing mortgage documents
- executing and recording other legal documents

In addition, a legal description provides a basis for court rulings on encroachments and easements.

The three accepted methods of legally describing parcels of real estate are:
- metes and bounds
- rectangular survey system, or government survey method
- recorded plat method, or lot and block method

Since the metes and bounds method preceded the inception of the rectangular survey system, the older East Coast states generally employ metes and bounds descriptions. States in the Midwest and West predominantly use the rectangular survey system. Some states combine methods.

METES AND BOUNDS

A metes and bounds description identifies the boundaries of a parcel of real estate using reference points, distances, and angles. The description always identifies an enclosed area by starting at an origination point, called point of beginning, or POB, and returning to the POB at the end of the description. A metes and bounds description *must return to the POB in order to be valid*.

The term "metes" refers to distance and direction, and the term "bounds" refers to fixed reference points, or monuments and landmarks, which may be natural and artificial. Natural landmarks include trees, rocks, rivers, and lakes. Artificial landmarks are typically surveyor stakes.

Many states use metes and bounds description to describe properties within the rectangular survey system.

A metes and bounds description begins with an identification of the city, county, and state where the property is located. Next, it identifies the POB and describes the distance and direction from the POB to the first monument, and then to subsequent monuments that *define the property's enclosed perimeter*.

Sample Metes and Bounds Description

A parcel of land located in Bucks County, Pennsylvania, having the following description: commencing at the intersection of the south line of Route 199 and the middle of Flint Creek, thence southeasterly along the center thread of Flint Creek 410 feet, more or less, to the willow tree landmark, thence north 65 degrees west 500 feet, more or less to the east line of Dowell Road, thence north 2 degrees east 200 feet, more or less, along the east line of Dowell Road to the south line of Route 199, thence north 90 degrees east 325 feet, more or less, along the south line of Route 199 to the point of beginning.

THE RECTANGULAR SURVEY SYSTEM

The federal government developed the **rectangular survey system**, or government survey method, to simplify and standardize property descriptions as a replacement for the cumbersome and often inaccurate metes and bounds method. The system was further modified to facilitate the transfer of large quantities of government-owned western lands to private parties.

To institute the system, all affected land was surveyed using latitude (east-west) and longitude (north-south) lines. The object was to create uniform grids of squares, called townships, which would have equal size and be given a numerical reference for identification.

The rectangular survey system works well for describing properties that are square or rectangular in shape, since these can be described as fractions of sections. However, for an irregular shape, such as a triangle, the rectangular system is inadequate as a method of legal description. The full description has to include a metes and bounds or lot and block description.

The survey grid

The following exhibit shows a portion of the rectangular survey system.

A Sample Survey Grid

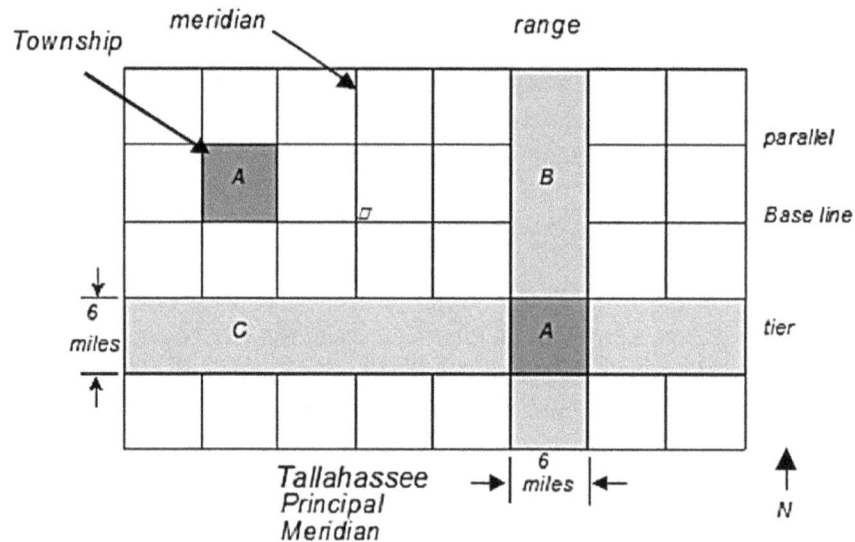

Meridian. The north-south, longitudinal lines on the survey grid are meridians. The principal meridian is the single designated meridian for identifying townships in the principal meridian's geographical "jurisdiction." There are 37 principal meridians in the national survey. In the exhibit, the principal meridian is the Tallahassee Principal Meridian.

Parallel. The east-west, latitudinal lines are called parallels. The base parallel or base line is the designated line for identifying townships. There is a base parallel for each principal meridian
Range. The north-south area between consecutive meridians is called a range. The area labeled "B" in the exhibit is a range. A range is identified by its relationship to the principal meridian. All ranges are six miles wide.

Tier. The east-west area between two parallels is called a tier, or a township strip. The area marked "C" in the exhibit is a tier. A tier is identified by its relationship to the base parallel. All tiers are six miles wide.

Township. A township is the area enclosed by the intersection of two consecutive meridians and two consecutive parallels, as the shaded square marked "A" in the exhibit illustrates. Since the parallels and meridians are six miles apart, a township is a square with six miles on each side. Its area is therefore 36 square miles.

Sections of a township

The rectangular survey system divides a township into thirty-six squares called sections. Each side of a section is one mile in length. Thus the area of a section is one square mile, or 640 acres.

As the following exhibit illustrates, the sections in a township are numbered sequentially starting with Section 1 in the northeast corner, proceeding east to west across the top row, continuing from west to east across the next lower row, and so on, alternately, ending with Section 36 in the southeast corner.

Sections of a Township

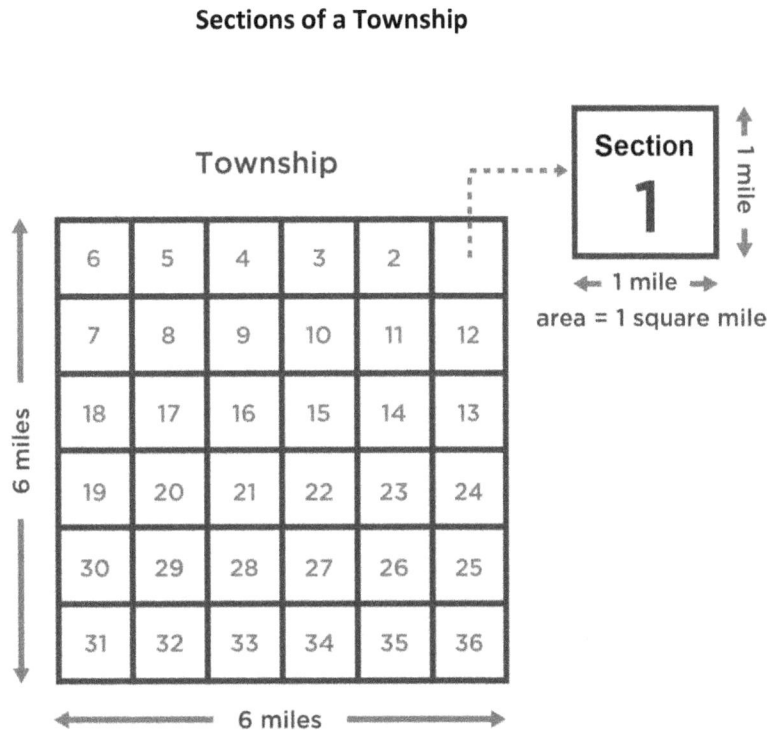

Township

6	5	4	3	2	1
7	8	9	10	11	12
18	17	16	15	14	13
19	20	21	22	23	24
30	29	28	27	26	25
31	32	33	34	35	36

6 miles
6 miles

Section
1

1 mile
1 mile
area = 1 square mile

Fractions of a section

A section of a township can be divided into fractions as the following exhibit shows

Fractions of Sections and Acreage

1 section = 640 acres

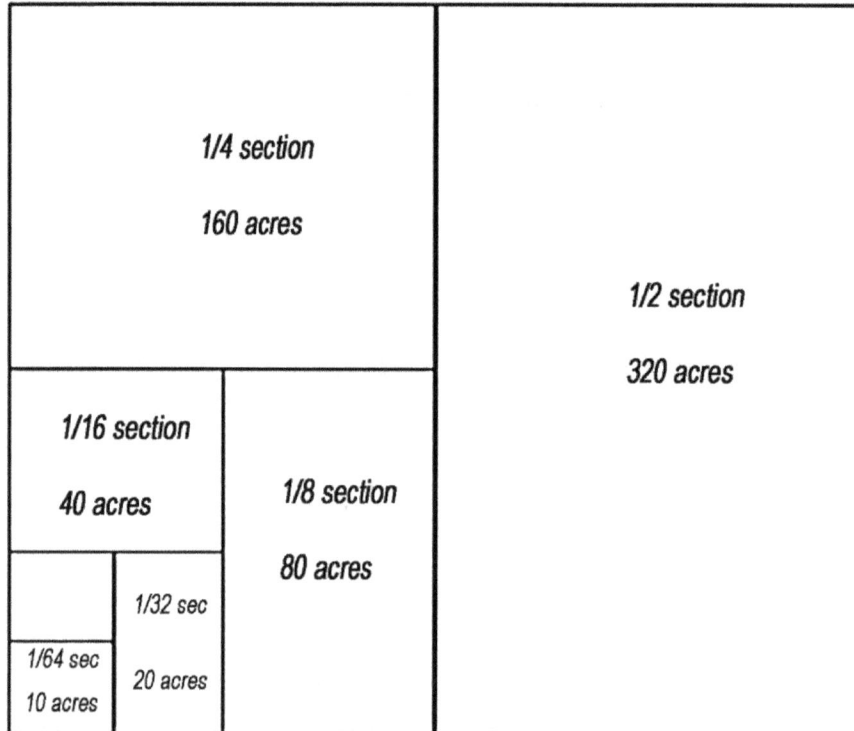

1/4 section 160 acres	1/2 section 320 acres
1/16 section — 40 acres / 1/8 section — 80 acres 1/64 sec — 10 acres / 1/32 sec — 20 acres	

Converting section fractions to acres

The size in acres of a subsection of a township is a fraction of 640 acres, since there are 640 acres in a section.

For example, the SW 1/4 of a section is one quarter section. Thus, its acreage is one quarter of 640, or 160 acres. Going further, the E 1/2 of the SW 1/4 is one half of that one quarter, or 80 acres. The E 1/2 of the SW 1/4 of the SW ¼ is 20 acres.

To calculate the acreage of a parcel from its legal description, multiply the fractional portion of the section in the description times 640 acres. Thus, if the property to be measured is the NE ¼ of the section, multiple the ¼ times 640, or 120 acres.

If a parcel is described as a portion of a portion of a section, such as the NW ¼ of the East ½ of a section, multiply the fractional portions together, then multiply that number times 640 acres. Thus the NW ¼ of the East ½ of a section is ¼ times ½ times 640 acres, or 1/8 times 640, or 80 acres.

DESCRIBING ELEVATION

Datums. To describe property located above or below the earth's surface, such as the air rights of a condominium, a surveyor must know the property's elevation. Standard elevation reference points, called datums, have been established throughout the country. The original datum was defined by the U.S. Geological Survey as mean sea level at New York harbor. A surveyor uses a datum as an official elevation point to describe the height or depth of a property. If, for example, the datum for an area is a point 100 feet above sea level, all surveys in the area will indicate elevation as a distance above or below 100 feet above sea level.

Benchmarks. In many cases it is impractical for a surveyor to rely on a single datum for an entire surveying area. To simplify matters, surveyors have identified local elevation markers, called benchmarks, to provide reference elevations for nearby properties. Once a benchmark is registered, it provides a valid reference point for surveying other elevations in the immediate area.

MEAURING LAND AREA

Measuring land area is generally achievable by calculating the area of geometrical shapes – squares, triangles, trapezoids, and in some cases circles.

To find the area of an irregular tract, try dividing it into triangles, rectangles, squares or trapezoids and calculate the areas of those parts; the area of the whole parcel is then the sum of the areas of all of its subparts. The formula for the area of a four-sided tract is **base times height** as explained below. A triangle is **base times height divided by 2**.

Base and height

1. Formulas for area of three- and four-sided shapes use a product of base and height. In the formulas, a represents area, b represents base, h represents height, SF represents square feet.
2. The base of a triangle, square, or rectangle may be any side; a trapezoid has two bases, its two parallel sides.
3. The height of a triangle is the length of a perpendicular line from the base to the triangle's opposite point. Height in a square, rectangle or trapezoid is the length of a line which is perpendicular to the base line(s).

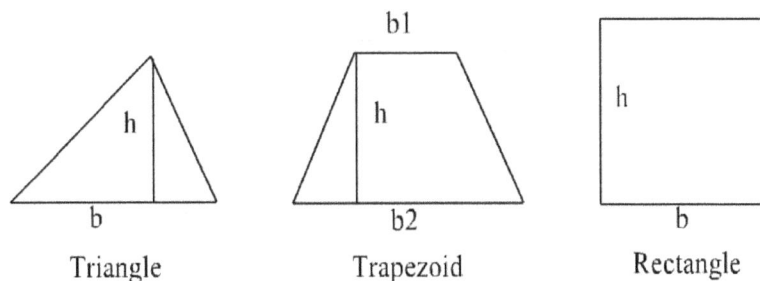

Triangle   Trapezoid   Rectangle

Area of a square or rectangle

1. Formula: area (a) = base (b) x height (h) a = b x h
2. Example: A square measures 3 feet on each side.
   Its area is: 3 x 3 = 9 SF

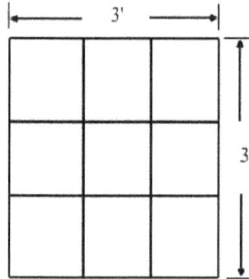

Area of a triangle

1. Formula: a = b x h2
2. Example: A triangle has a 20' base and a 4' height. It's area is:

$$a = \frac{20 \times 4}{2} = 40 \ SF$$

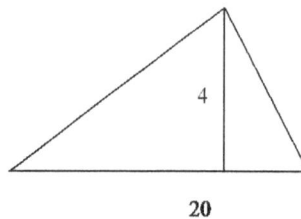

20

Area of a trapezoid

1. Formula: a = a (b1+ b2)2
2. Example: A trapezoid's two bases are 10' and 15'.
   It's area is $a = \dfrac{7\ (10 + 15)}{2} = 87.5 \ SF$

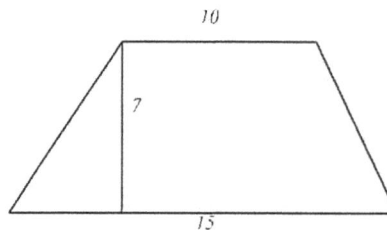

Using the formulas, then, the area of a rectangular lot measuring 55' on two sides and 130' on two sides would be 55' (base) x 130' (height), or 7,150 square feet.

MEASURING LIVING AREA

Understanding living area measurements in residential brokerage is absolutely critical, since the price of any home for sale is a function of how much living area there is. Further, the standards for measuring and publicly quoting a property's living area must take into account that some improved area is actually occupiable, or livable, while other areas are not. For that reason, the concept of living area has been established so that consumers can rely on just how large the livable portion of a given property is.

Living area value considerations

Consider the purchase of a farm property. There is the house, the barn, a silo, and several sheds. What is the living area upon which the property's price will be largely determined? How does one value the silo and the shed? How much more or less is the value of the barn? Finally, what is the living area of the house? Do you include the porch and the attic in the calculations? What about the garage?

To answer these questions, appraisers, brokers, and regulatory jurisdictions have developed standards that define what elements are includable or excludable from a property's living area, or, technically, its gross living area. Once these standards are accepted in a market, buyers and sellers can reliably quote prices for living area – then tack on various values for improvements that add to the value as separately valued pieces. But in every instance, deriving the living area is the foundational factoid for quoting the property's value.

What follows is a generalized profiling of living area standards and considerations. They are based on guidelines developed and promulgated by the North Carolina Real Estate Commission in its publication entitled "Residential Square Footage Guidelines." This can be accessed via the following link:

https://www.ncrec.gov/Brochures/Measurementbooklet2013.pdf

NCREC living area standards

- **Heated**. To be considered living area, the space must be heated by a permanent, immovable system that heats year-round. Cannot be a portable heater or fireplace
- **Finished**. The improved area must be finished with completed walls, flooring, and ceiling with a minimum of 7' height. (Some exceptions)
- **Directly accessible to / from other living area.** Via hallway or door.
- **Attics**. Includable as living area if heated, finished, accessible. May require a ceiling height adjustment if walls are slanted
- **Basements**. Again, countable if improved; may require a below-grade deduction
- Hallways, closets, furnace room, laundry room, stairs – all are includable in living area
- Decks, balconies, porches, garages, carports – not includable as living area

NCREC measuring standards

- measurements must be "reasonably right" meaning within 5% margin of error
- living area measurements are based on **exterior measurements** with the exception of condominiums which are based on **interior measurements**.
- Measure area by measuring each exterior wall and develop a sketch of the improvement. Identify living and *other* area. Then, inspect the property and identify areas that do not qualify as living area.
- Derive the living area from the sketch by multiplying length times width of each space; add six inches to account for any wall
- Licensees are generally expected to be able to accurately measure and derive living area. However, they are also allowed to rely on previous area estimates.
- If a given room in the house was not permitted (built without regulatory permission), the licensee may include the area in the living area total, but the lack of a permit should be noted in the transaction documents.

Taking all considerations into account, the accurate estimation of living area is a cornerstone of the licensee's repertoire of specialized skills. Further, generating an accurate distinction between improved area and living area – as well as generating accurate measurements and representations of lot size – is of considerable benefit to the client in delivering professional service.

SNAPSHOT REVIEW:

Unit 13: MEASURING REAL PROPERTY

METHODS OF LEGAL DESCRIPTION

- accurately locates and identifies boundaries of subject parcel to degree acceptable by courts of law in state where property is located

- provides sufficient data for a surveyor to locate the parcel

- required for creating valid deed; mortgage documents; recording legal documents

METES AND BOUNDS

- identifies the boundaries of a parcel of real estate using reference points, distances, and angles

THE RECTANGULAR SURVEY SYSTEM

- government survey method

- standardize property descriptions as replacement for metes and bounds method

- for irregular shape, such as a triangle, rectangular system is inadequate

The survey grid

- **Meridian.** North-south, longitudinal lines on the survey grid

- **Parallel.** East-west, latitudinal lines

- **Tier.** East-west area between 2 parallels

- **Township.** Area enclosed by intersection of 2 consecutive meridians and 2 consecutive parallels

Sections of a township

- rectangular survey system divides township into 36 squares called sections

Fractions of a section

- sections can be divided into fractions

Converting section fractions to acres

- size in acres of subsection of township is fraction of 640 acres

DESCRIBING ELEVATION

- **Datums.** Standard elevation reference points

- **Benchmarks.** Local elevation markers

MEASURING LAND AREA

- calculating area of geometrical shapes – squares, triangles, trapezoids, circles

Base and height

- formulas for area of 3 and 4 sided shapes use product of base and height

Area of square or rectangle

- area = base x height

Area of a triangle

- area = base x height/2

Area of a trapezoid

- area = a (b1+b2)/2

MEASURING LIVING AREA

Living area value considerations

- appraisers, brokers, regulatory jurisdictions have standards defining what elements are includable/excludable from living area

NCREC living area standards

- **Heated.** Space must be heated by permanent, immovable system that heats year-round

- **Finished.** Finished with completed walls, flooring, ceiling with minimum of 7' height

- **Directly accessible to/from other living area.** Via hallway or door

- **Attics.** Includable as living area if heated, finished, accessible

- **Basements.** Countable if improved

NCREC measuring standards

- measurements must be "reasonably right" within 5% margin of error
- based on exterior measurements; condominiums based on interior measurements

- licensees expected to measure and derive living area; allowed to rely on previous area estimates

===

Check Your Understanding Quiz:

Unit 13: Measuring Real Property

Carefully read each question and provide your best answer based on what you learned in this module. Then check your answers against the Answer Key which immediately follows the quiz questions.

1. What are the three accepted methods of legally describing parcels?

   a. Metes and bounds, rectangular survey system, and lot and block method
   b. Surveying, circle method, and boundary method
   c. Metes and bounds, diamond survey system, and sketch method
   d. Drafting, survey system, and lot and block method

2. The east-west area between two parallels is called a _____.

   a. parallel.
   b. strip.
   c. tier.
   d. meridian.

3. How many acres are in a section?

   a. 500 acres
   b. 640 acres
   c. 370 acres
   d. 750 acres

4. Standard elevation reference points are called _____.

   a. benchmarks.
   b. metes.
   c. bounds.
   d. datums.

5. NCREC states that living area measurements must be within a ___ margin of error.

   a. 10%
   b. 5%
   c. 7%
   d. 3%

6. Which legal description method identifies boundaries of a parcel by using reference points, distances, and angles?

   a. Metes and bounds
   b. Lot and block method
   c. Survey method
   d. Recorded plat method

7. Which system was developed by the federal government to standardize property descriptions?

   a. Metes and bounds
   b. Lot method
   c. Rectangular survey system
   d. Block method

8. The north-south, longitudinal lines on a survey grid are called _____.

   a. tiers.
   b. townships.
   c. laterals.
   d. meridians.

9. Surveys often rely on _____ to provide reference elevations for nearby properties.

   a. datums
   b. tiers
   c. benchmarks
   d. posts

10. What does a metes and bounds description begin with?

   a. Point of beginning
   b. Identification of the city, county, and state
   c. The direction from a landmark
   d. Property's perimeter

Exercise Workshop -- Unit 13: Measuring Real Property

Exercise 13-1. Measuring Land, Lots, & Living Area

Synopsis:

In this exercise, the student will demonstrate their understanding of how to figure out how many acres are in a legal description and how many square feet are in a parcel of land.

Instructions:

Solve each problem below to determine the size of the lots or land.

Exercise:

1. Determine the number of acres in the following legal description:

    NW ¼ of the NE ¼ of the SW ¼ of Section 13, Tier 3 North, Range 4 West

2. Determine the number of square feet in the following legal description (43,560 SF in one acre):

    NE ½ of the NE ¼ of the SE ¼ of Section 2, T5N, R6W

3. A piece of land is rectangular in shape. The lot is 250 ft x 500 ft. What is the area of the lot?

4. A piece of land is triangular in shape. The lot has a base of 300 feet and a height of 50 feet. What is the area of the lot?

5. A piece of land is a trapezoid. The bases of the lot are 250 feet and 150 feet, with a height of 30 feet. What is the area of the lot?

6. Sally is looking at a house to rent and asks the real estate agent for information on the house. The agent sent her the room dimension: Living room 15' x 16'; Dining room 10' x 10'; Kitchen 10' x 12'; Bedroom #1 15' x 19', Bedroom #2 10' x 12';Bedroom #3 10' x

10'; Bedroom #4 10' x 11'; Bathroom #1 8' x 5'; Bathroom #2 5' x 5'; Bathroom #3 5' x 5'. There is a front porch which is 5' x 8'; a screened-in back porch that is 10' x 15'; and, a garage which measures 20' x 25'.

What is the total square footage?

What is the total square living area?

Unit 14: Real Property Valuation

Unit 14: Real Property Valuation – Learning Objectives

When the student has completed Unit 14, he or she will be able to:

> **1. Describe how the economic principles of supply and demand impact real property values and real estate market cycles**
>
> **2. Identify the key differentiations between an appraisal and a broker's opinion of value**
>
> **3. Summarize the valuation principles of substitution, contribution, depreciation and obsolescence**
>
> **4. Describe the process of completing a Comparative Market Analysis and summarize the uses of the value estimate it derives**
>
> **5. Summarize how to adjust comparables given differences between the comp and the subject; summarize how to reconcile all the CMA's adjustments**

THE AMERICAN MARKET SYSTEM

The valuation of real property is one of the most fundamental activities in the real estate business. Its role is particularly critical in the transfer of real property since the value of a parcel establishes the general price range for the principal parties to negotiate.

In understanding value and pricing, it is important to appreciate the underlying determinants of value: supply and demand. These are the fundamental economic forces interacting in the market that drive the upward and downward movement of prices.

Supply and demand

The goal of an economic system is to produce and distribute a supply of goods and services to satisfy the demand of its constituents. Economic activity therefore centers on the production, distribution and sale of goods and services to meet consumer demand.

- **Supply** is the quantity of a product or service available for sale, lease, or trade at any given time.

- **Demand** is the quantity of a product or service that is desired for purchase, lease, or trade at any given time.

The interplay of supply and demand is what makes an economy work: consumers demand goods and services; suppliers and sellers produce and distribute the goods and services for a negotiated price.

Price and value

The price mechanism. In addition to supply and demand, the other critical component of an economic system is the price mechanism, or simply, price. A price is the amount of money or other asset that a buyer has agreed to pay and a seller has agreed to accept to complete the exchange of a good or service. It is a quantification of the value of an item traded.

Price in this context means the final trading price; it is not the preliminary asking price of the seller nor the initial bidding price of the purchaser. Asking and bidding prices are pricing positions in a negotiation between the parties prior to the exchange. The true price of an item or service is the final number the parties agree to.

Value and value determinants. Price is not something of value in itself. It is only a number that quantifies value. The economic issue underlying the interplay of supply and demand is, how do trading parties arrive at the value of a good or service as indicated by the price?

Consider consumer demand for air conditioners. Why do air conditioners have value? How do they command the price they do?

The value of something is based on the answers to four questions:
- How much do I desire it?
- How useful is it?
- How scarce is it?
- Am I able to pay for it?

Desire. One determinant of value is how dear the item is to the purchaser. Returning to the air conditioner example, the question becomes "how much do I desire to be cool, dry, and comfortable?" To a person who lives in the tropics, it is safe to say that air conditioning is more valuable than a heating system. It is also safe to say the opposite is true for residents of northern Alaska.

Utility. The second determinant of value is the product's ability to do the job. Can the air conditioner satisfy my need to stay cool? How cool does it make my house? Does it even work properly? Of course, I won't pay as much if it is old or ineffectual.

Scarcity. The third critical element of value is a product's availability in relation to demand. The air conditioner is quite valuable if there are only five units in the entire city and everyone is hot. On the other hand, the value of an air conditioner goes down if there are ten thousand units for sale in a 500-person market.

Purchasing power. A fourth component of value is the consumer's ability to pay for the item. If one cannot afford to buy the air conditioner, the value of the air conditioner is diminished, since it is financially out of reach. If all air conditioners are too expensive, consumers are forced to consider alternatives such as ceiling fans.

In the marketplace, the relative presence or absence of the four elements of value is constantly changing due to innumerable factors. Since price is a reflection of the total of all value factors at any time, changes in the underlying factors of value trigger changes in price.

REAL ESTATE MARKET DYNAMICS

As an economic commodity, real estate is bought, sold, traded, and leased as a product within a real estate market.

Economic characteristics of real estate

Real estate, like other products and services, is:

- subject to the laws of supply and demand
- governed in the market by the price mechanism
- influenced by the producer's costs to bring the product to market
- influenced by the determinants of value: utility, scarcity, desire, and purchasing power

Distinguishing features. In comparison with other economic products and services, real estate has certain unique traits. These include:

- **Inherent product value**

  Land is a scarce resource as well as a required factor of production. Like gold and silver, it has both inherent value and utility value.

- **Unique appeal of product**

  Since no two parcels of real estate can be alike (each has a different location), every parcel of real property has its own appeal. Likewise, no two parcels of real estate can have exactly the same value, except by coincidence.

- **Demand must come to the supply**

  Since real property cannot be moved, real property investors and users must come to the supply. This creates risk, because if demand drops, the supply cannot be transported to a higher demand market.

- **Illiquid**

  Real estate is a relatively illiquid economic product, meaning it cannot always be readily sold for cash. Since it is a large, long-term investment that has no exact duplicate, buyers must go through a complex process to evaluate and purchase the right parcel of real estate.

- **Slow to respond to changes**

  Real estate is relatively slow to respond to market imbalances. Because new construction is a large-scale, time-consuming process, the market is slow to respond to increases in demand. The market is similarly slow to respond to sharp declines in demand, since the product cannot be moved and sold elsewhere. Instead, owners must wait out slow periods and simply hope for the best.

- **Decentralized, local market**

    A real property cannot be shipped to a large, central real estate marketplace. Real estate markets are thus local in nature and highly susceptible to swings in the local economy.

Real estate supply and demand

Supply. In real estate, supply is the amount of property available for sale or lease at any given time. The units of supply used to quantify the amount of property available differ for different categories of property. These supply units, by property type, are:

- residential: dwelling units
- commercial and industrial: square feet
- agricultural: acreage

Factors influencing supply. In addition to the influences of demand and the underlying determinants of value, real estate supply responds to

- development costs, particularly labor
- availability of financing
- investment returns
- a community's master plan
- government police powers and regulation

Demand. Real estate demand is the amount of property buyers and tenants wish to acquire by purchase, lease or trade at any given time. Units of demand, by property classification, are:

- residential: households
- commercial and industrial: square feet
- agricultural: acreage

Supply and demand interaction. Real estate supply and demand, like supply and demand for other economic products, interact in the marketplace to produce price movements.

Real Estate Supply-Demand Cycle

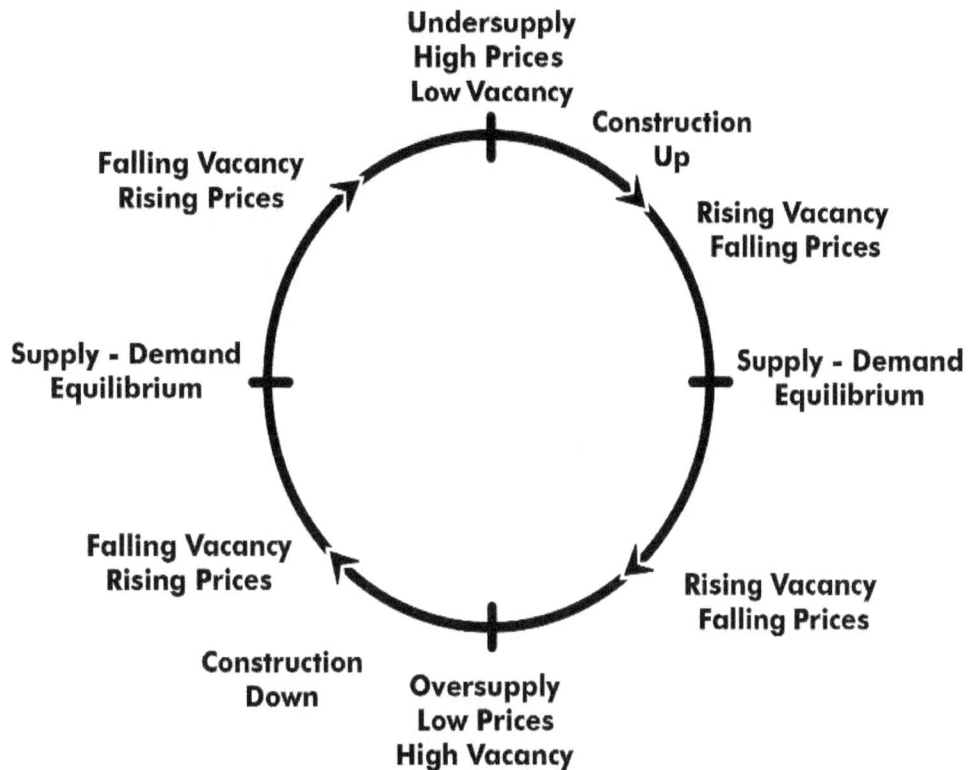

Undersupply
High Prices
Low Vacancy

Construction
Up

Falling Vacancy
Rising Prices

Rising Vacancy
Falling Prices

Supply - Demand
Equilibrium

Supply - Demand
Equilibrium

Falling Vacancy
Rising Prices

Rising Vacancy
Falling Prices

Construction
Down

Oversupply
Low Prices
High Vacancy

APPRAISING MARKET VALUE

Market value

Understanding market economics and supply and demand interaction gives the licensee a solid foundation for estimating market value and pricing residential properties. The complexity in valuation, however, is that there are numerous types of value – leasehold, insured, book value, mortgage value, depreciated value – to name a few. What we are after in this context of residential valuation is the type of value referred to as market value. "Market value" is the quantification that residential licensees are after in valuing properties and understanding prices in a market.

Market value validity criteria. There is a specific set of criteria for defining and validating market value, as follows:

Market value is an opinion of the price that a willing seller and willing buyer would probably agree on for a property at a given time if:

- the transaction is a cash transaction
- the property is exposed on the open market for a reasonable period
- buyer and seller have full information about market conditions and about potential uses

159

- there is no abnormal pressure on either party to complete the transaction
- buyer and seller are not related (it is an "arm's length" transaction)
- title is marketable and conveyable by the seller
- the price is a "normal consideration," that is, it does not include hidden influences such as special financing deals, concessions, terms, services, fees, credits, costs, or other types of consideration.

Market price. The market price, as opposed to market value, is what a property actually sells for. Market price should theoretically be the same as market value if all the conditions essential for market value were present. Market price, however, may not reflect the analysis of comparables and of investment value that an estimate of market value includes.

Broker's opinion of value (BPO). A broker's opinion of value may resemble an appraisal, but it differs from an appraisal in that it is not necessarily performed by a disinterested third party or licensed professional and it generally uses only a limited form of one of the three appraisal approaches. In addition, the opinion is not subject to regulation, nor does it follow any particular professional standards.

Value principles underlying residential valuation

To identify residential market value, appraisers and brokers principally rely on two principles of value: *substitution and contribution*.

Substitution. According to the principle of substitution, a buyer will pay no more for a property than the buyer would have to pay for an equally desirable and available substitute property. For example, if three houses for sale are essentially similar in size, quality and location, a potential buyer is unlikely to choose the one that is priced significantly higher than the other two. This principle is actively applied in developing a broker's competitive market analysis, or CMA. Numerous properties are compared to the subject property using the assumption that buyers will not pay more for a given property than they would for a similar property located elsewhere.

Contribution. The principal of contribution focuses on the degree to which a particular improvement affects market value of the overall property. In essence, the contribution of the improvement is equal to the change in market value that the addition of the improvement causes.

For example, adding a bathroom to a house may contribute an additional $15,000 to the appraised value. Thus, the contribution of the bathroom is $15,000. Note that an improvement's contribution to value has little to do with the improvement's cost. The foregoing bathroom may have cost $5,000 or $20,000. Contribution is what the market recognizes as the change in value, not what an item cost.

If continuous improvements are added to a property, it is possible that, at some point, the cost of adding improvements to a property no longer contributes a corresponding increase in the value of the property. When this occurs, the property suffers from diminishing marginal return, where the costs to improve exceed contribution.

ESTIMATING RESIDENTIAL PROPERTY VALUE

The sales comparison approach, also known as the market data approach, is used for almost all properties. It also serves as the basis for a broker's opinion of value. As stated previously, it is based on the principle of substitution-- that a buyer will pay no more for the subject property than would be sufficient to purchase a comparable property-- and contribution-- that specific characteristics add value to a property.

The sales comparison approach is widely used because it takes into account the subject property's specific amenities in relation to competing properties. In addition, because of the currency of its data, the approach incorporates present market realities.

Steps in the approach

The sales comparison approach consists of comparing sale prices of recently sold properties that are comparable with the subject, and making dollar adjustments to the price of each comparable to account for competitive differences with the subject. After identifying the adjusted value of each comparable, the appraiser weighs the reliability of each comparable and the factors underlying how the adjustments were made. The weighting yields a final value range based on the most reliable factors in the analysis.

Steps in the Sales Comparison Approach

1. *Identify comparable sales.*
2. *Compare comparables to the subject and make adjustments to comparables.*
3. *Weight values indicated by adjusted comparables for the final value estimate of the subject.*

Identifying comparables

To qualify as a comparable, a property must:

- resemble the subject in size, shape, design, utility and location
- have sold recently, generally within six months of the appraisal
- have sold in an arm's-length transaction

An appraiser considers three to six comparables, and usually includes at least three in the appraisal report.

Appraisers have specific guidelines within the foregoing criteria for selecting comparables, many of which are set by secondary market organizations such as FNMA. For example, to qualify as a comparable for a mortgage loan appraisal, a property might have to be located within one mile of the subject. Or perhaps the size of the comparable must be within a certain percentage of improved area in relation to the subject.

The time-of-sale criterion is important because transactions that occurred too far in the past will not reflect appreciation or recent changes in market conditions.

An arm's length sale involves objective, disinterested parties who are presumed to have negotiated a market price for the property. If the sale of a house occurred between a father and a daughter, for example, one might assume that the transaction did not reflect market value.

Principal sources of data for generating the sales comparison are tax records, title records, and the local multiple listing service.

Adjusting comparables

The appraiser must adjust the values of the comparables to account for competitive differences with the subject property. Note that the sale prices of the comparables are known, while the value and price of the subject are not. Therefore, adjustments can be made only to the comparables' prices, not to the subject's. Adjustments are made to the comparables in the form of a value deduction or a value addition.

Adding or deducting value. If the comparable is better than the subject in some characteristic, an amount is *deducted* from the sale price of the comparable. This accounts for the value discrepancy – if for example the comparable did not have that extra bedroom, it would have sold for less – so make a deduction so that the subject and the comp are equalized.

If the comparable is inferior to the subject in some characteristic, an amount is *added* to the price of the comparable. This adjustment equalizes the subject's competitive advantage in this area. Note that the subject is never adjusted!

Key adjustment criteria. The principal factors for comparison and adjustment are time of sale, location, physical characteristics, and transaction characteristics.

- **time of sale**

  An adjustment may be made if market conditions, market prices, or financing availability have changed significantly since the date of the comparable's sale. Most often, this adjustment is to account for appreciation.

- **location**

  An adjustment may be made if there are differences between the comparable's location and the subject's, including neighborhood desirability and appearance, zoning restrictions, and general price levels.

- **physical characteristics**

  Adjustments may be made for marketable differences between the comparable's and subject's lot size, square feet of livable area (or other appropriate measure for the property type), number of rooms, layout, age, condition, construction type and quality, landscaping, and special amenities.

- **transaction characteristics**

  An adjustment may be made for such differences as mortgage loan terms, mortgage assumability, and owner financing.

Weighting comparables.

Adding and subtracting the appropriate adjustments to the sale price of each comparable results in an adjusted price for the comparables that indicates the value of the subject. The last step in the approach is to perform a weighted analysis of the indicated values of each comparable. The appraiser, in other words, must identify which comparable values are more indicative of the subject and which are less indicative.

An appraiser primarily relies on experience and judgment to weight comparables. There is no formula for selecting a value from within the range of all comparables analyzed. However, there are three quantitative guidelines: the total number of adjustments; the amount of a single adjustment; and the net value change of all adjustments.

As a rule, *the fewer the total number of adjustments, the smaller the adjustment amounts, and the less the total adjustment amount, the more reliable the comparable.*

Broker's comparative market analysis

A broker or associate who is attempting to establish a listing price or range of prices for a property uses a scaled-down version of the appraiser's sales comparison approach called a comparative market analysis, or **CMA** (also called a competitive market analysis). While the CMA serves a useful purpose in setting general price ranges, brokers and agents need to exercise caution in presenting a CMA as an appraisal, which it is not. Two important distinctions between the two are objectivity and comprehensiveness.

First, the broker is not unbiased: he or she is motivated by the desire to obtain a listing, which can lead one to distort the estimated price. Secondly, the broker's CMA is not comprehensive: the broker does not usually consider the full range of data about market conditions and comparable sales that the appraiser must consider and document. Therefore, the broker's opinion will be less reliable than the appraiser's.

The following is a case illustration of a comparative market analysis.   A broker is estimating market value for a certain house. Four comparables are adjusted to find an indicated value for the subject. The grid which follows the property and market data shows the adjustments for the differences between the four comparables and the subject.

CMA Case Illustration:

Data

Subject property:

> 8 rooms-- 3 bedrooms, two baths, kitchen, living room, family room; 2,000 square feet of gross living area; 2-car attached garage; landscaping is good. Construction is frame with aluminum siding.

Comparable A:

> Sold for 1,000,000 within previous month; conventional financing at current rates; located in subject's neighborhood with similar locational advantages; house approximately same age as subject; lot size smaller than subject; view similar to subject; design less appealing than subject's; construction similar to subject; condition similar to subject; 7 rooms-- two bedrooms,

one bath; 1,900 square feet of gross living area; 2-car attached garage; landscaping similar to subject.

Comparable B:

Sold for 1,200,000 within previous month; conventional financing at current rates; located in subject's neighborhood with similar locational advantages; house six years newer than subject; lot size smaller than subject; view is better than the subject's; design is more appealing than subject's; construction (brick and frame) better than subject's; better condition than subject; 10 rooms--four bedrooms, three baths; 2,300 square feet of gross living area; 2-car attached garage; landscaping similar to subject.

Comparable C:

Sold for 1,150,000 within previous month; conventional financing at current rates; located in subject's neighborhood with similar locational advantages; house five years older than subject; lot size larger than subject; view similar to subject; design and appeal similar to subject's; construction similar to subject; condition similar to subject; 8 rooms-- three bedrooms, two baths; 2,000 square feet of gross living area; 2-car attached garage; landscaping similar to subject.

Comparable D:

Sold for 1,090,000 within previous month; conventional financing at current rates; located in a neighborhood close to subject's, but more desirable than subject's; house approximately same age as subject; lot size same as subject; view similar to subject; design less appealing than subject's; construction (frame) poorer than subject's; poorer condition than subject; 7 rooms-- two bedrooms, one and one half baths; 1,900 square feet of gross living area; 2-car attached garage; landscaping similar to subject.

Sales Comparison Approach Illustration:

Adjustments

	Subject	A	B	C	D
Sale price		1,000,000	1,200,000	1,150,000	1,090,000
Financing terms		standard	standard	standard	standard
Sale date	NOW	equal	equal	equal	equal
Location		equal	equal	equal	-20,000
Age		equal	-12,000	+10,000	equal
Lot size		+10,000	+10,000	-10,000	equal
Site/view		equal	-10,000	equal	equal
Design/appeal		+10,000	-12,000	equal	+5,000
Construction quality	good	equal	-30,000	equal	+10,000
Condition	good	equal	-50,000	equal	+20,000
No. of rooms	8				
No. of bedrooms	3	+5,000	-5,000	equal	+5,000
No. of baths	2	+10,000	-15,000	equal	+5,000
Gross living area	2,000	+10,000	-20,000	equal	+10,000
Other space					
Garage	2 car/attd.	equal	equal	equal	equal
Other improvements					
Landscaping	good	equal	equal	equal	equal
Net adjustments		+45,000	-144,000	0	+35,000
Indicated value	1,120,000	1,045,000	1,056,000	1,150,000	1,125,000

Sales Comparison Approach Illustration:

Analysis and Reconciliation

Analysis

For comparable A, the appraiser has made additions to the lot value, design, number of bedrooms and baths, and for gross living area. This accounts for the comparable's deficiencies in these areas relative to the subject. A total of five adjustments amount to $45,000, or 4.5% of the purchase price.

For comparable B, the appraiser has deducted values for age, site, design, construction quality, condition, bedrooms, baths, and living area. This accounts for the comparable's superior qualities relative to the subject. The only addition is the lot size, since the subject's is larger. A total of nine adjustments amount to $144,000, or 12% of the sale price.

For comparable C, the appraiser has added value for the age and deducted value for the lot size. The two adjustments offset one another for a net adjustment of zero.

For comparable D, one deduction has been made for the comparable's superior location. This is offset by six additions reflecting the various areas where the comparable is inferior to the subject. A total of seven adjustments amount to $35,000, or 3.2% of the sale price.

Reconciliation

In view of all adjusted comparables, the appraiser developed a final indication of value of $1,120,000 for the subject. Underlying this conclusion is the fact that Comparable C, since it only has two minor adjustments which offset each other, it is by far the best indicator of value. Comparable D might be the second-best indicator, since the net adjustments are very close to the sale price. Comparable A might be the third best indicator, since it has the second fewest number of total adjustments. Comparable B is the least reliable indicator, since there are numerous adjustments, three of which are of a significant amount. In addition, Comparable B is questionable altogether as a comparable, since total adjustments alter the sale price by 12%.

SNAPSHOT REVIEW:

Unit 14: REAL PROPERTY VALUATON

THE AMERICAN MARKET SYSTEM

Supply and demand

- produce supply of goods and services to satisfy demand of constituents

- supply is quantity of product/service available for sale, lease, trade

- demand is quantity of product/service desired for purchase, lease, trade

Price and value

- **The price mechanism.** Quantification of value of item traded

- **Value and value determinants.** Value based on desire, utility, scarcity, purchasing power

- **Desire.** How dear item is to purchaser

- **Utility.** Product's ability to do job

- **Scarcity.** Product's availability in relation to demand

- **Purchasing power.** Consumer's ability to pay for item

REAL ESTATE MARKET DYNAMICS

Economic characteristics of real estate

- subject to laws of supply/demand; governed by price mechanism; influenced by producer's cost and determinants of value

- **Distinguishing features.** Inherent product value; unique appeal of product; demand must come to supply; illiquid; slow to respond to changes; decentralized, local market

Real estate supply and demand

- **Supply.** Amount of property available for sale or lease

- **Factors influencing supply.** Development costs; financing; investment returns; community's master plan' government police power/regulations

- **Demand.** Amount of property buyers/tenants wish to acquire by purchase, lease, trade

- **Supply and demand interaction.** Supply and demand interact in marketplace to produce price movements

APPRAISING MARKET VALUE

Market value

- **Market value validity criteria.** Cash transaction; exposure to open market; market conditions; no abnormal pressure, etc.

- **Market price.** What property sells for

- **Broker's opinion of value (BPO).** May resemble appraisal; not necessarily performed by disinterested third party or licensed professional

Value principles underlying residential valuation

- **Substitution.** Buyer will pay no more for property than equally desirable and available substitute property

- **Contribution.** Focuses on degree to which particular improvement affects market value of overall property

ESTIMATING RESIDENTIAL PROPERTY VALUE

Steps in the approach

- identify comparable sales; compare comparables to subject; weight values indicated by adjusted comparables

Identifying comparables

- resemble subject size, shape, design, utility, location

- sold within 6 months of appraisal

- sold in arm's-length transaction

Adjusting comparables

- **Adding or deducting value.** If comparable is better than subject, an amount is deducted from sale price; if comparable is inferior, amount is added to sale price

- **Key adjustment criteria.** Time of sale; location; physical characteristics; transaction characteristics

Weighting comparables.

- the fewer the total number of adjustments, the smaller the adjustment amounts, and the less the total adjustment amount, the more reliable the comparable

Broker's comparative market analysis

- scaled-down version of appraiser's sales comparison approach

- broker is not unbiased

- broker does not usually consider full range of data about market conditions and comparable sales that appraiser must consider and document

Check Your Understanding Quiz:

Unit 14: Real Property Valuation

Carefully read each question and provide your best answer based on what you learned in this module. Then check your answers against the Answer Key which immediately follows the quiz questions.

1. The number of homes available for sale in a market at any given time is referred to as which of the following?

    a. New housing
    b. Supply
    c. Demand
    d. Total inventory

2. A product or property has a certain ability to perform or enable a given economic function. This principle of value is referred to as which of the following?

    a. Utility
    b. Scarcity
    c. Ability
    d. Power

3. What is the name of the principle that states a buyer will pay no more for a property than for an equally desirable and similar property?

    a. Estimation
    b. Contribution
    c. Duplication
    d. Substitution

4. In completing the adjustments for a competitive market analysis (CMA), if a comparable property is superior than the subject in some characteristic, an amount is _____.

    a. added to the sale price of the comparable.
    b. deducted from the sale price of the subject.
    c. deducted from the sale price of the comparable.
    d. added to the sale price of the subject.

5. The principal of _____ focuses on the degree to which a particular improvement affects the market value of the overall property.

    a. allocation
    b. contribution
    c. price fixing
    d. substitution

6. What is the name of the determinant of value that states how dear an item is to a purchaser?

   a. Desire
   b. Supply
   c. Demand
   d. Scarcity

7. The three critical components of the economic system are supply, demand, and _____.

   a. value.
   b. the price mechanism.
   c. consumerism.
   d. scarcity.

8. Which of the following is an opinion of price that is not subject to an appraisal license requirement?

   a. A residential appraisal
   b. A Broker's Opinion of Value (BPO)
   c. Assessor's value
   d. A mass appraisal

9. Which of the following is the final step in the Sales Comparison Approach?

   a. Identifying comparable sales
   b. Deducting values from the comparables
   c. Weighing the values indicated by adjusted comparables
   d. Comparing comparables to the subject

10. What is the amount a property actually sells for called?

   a. Its market price
   b. Its BPO value
   c. Its liquidation value
   d. Its appraised price

==

Exercise Workshop -- Unit 14: Real Property Valuation

Exercise 14-1. Developing a CMA

Synopsis:

In this exercise, the student will develop a CMA using the information given.

Instructions:

1. Set up a grid with the information about the subject property and the comps given.

2. Make adjustments to the comps as needed to come up with their adjusted value

3. Determine the range of pricing for the subject property.

Exercise:

Data

Subject property:

> 10 rooms-- 4 bedrooms, three baths, kitchen, living room, family room; 2,500 square feet of gross living area; 2-car attached garage; landscaping is good. Construction is frame with aluminum siding.

Comparable A:

> Sold for $850,000 within the previous month; conventional financing at current rates; located in subject's neighborhood; construction similar to the subject; condition similar to the subject; 9 rooms-- three bedrooms, two bath; 2,200 square feet of gross living area; 2-car attached garage; landscaping similar to the subject.

Comparable B:

> Sold for $900,000 within previous the month; conventional financing at current rates; located in subject's neighborhood; construction (brick and frame) better than subject's; 11 rooms--four bedrooms, four baths; 2,300 square feet of gross living area; 2-car attached garage; landscaping similar to the subject.

Comparable C:

> Sold for $750,000 within the previous month; conventional financing at current rates; located in subject's neighborhood construction similar to the subject; 8 rooms-- three bedrooms, two baths; 2,100 square feet of gross living area; 2-car attached garage; landscaping similar to the subject.

Comparable D:

Sold for $800,000 within the previous month; conventional financing at current rates; located in the same as the subject; construction (frame) poorer than subject's; 8 rooms-- two bedrooms, two bath; 1,900 square feet of gross living area; 2-car attached garage; landscaping similar to the subject.

The real estate agent estimates that a bedroom in this neighborhood is worth $5,000 and a bathroom is worth $3,000. Better construction is worth $50,000, and poorer construction is worth $25,000. Using just this information makes the required adjustments to the comparable properties. The standard adjustment for the living area, not including bedrooms and baths, is $2,000.

Sales Comparison Approach Illustration:

Adjustments

	Subject	Comp A	Comp B	Comp C	Comp D
Sales Price					
Financing Terms					
Sales Date					
Construction Quality					
No. of Room					
No. of BDRM					
No. of Baths					
Gross Living Area					
Adjust for Living Area					
Garage					
Landscaping					
Net Adjustments					
Value					

Module E: REAL ESTATE INVESTMENT AND TAXATION

Unit 15: Essential Characteristics of Real Estate Investments
Unit 16: Investment Analysis of Non-income Property
Unit 17: Investment Analysis of Income Property
Unit 18: Investment Performance Analysis

Module E Learning Objectives

Essential Characteristics of Real Estate Investments

> 1. Summarize the salient characteristics of a real estate investment in terms of risk and return, and the financial measurement components of taxable income, tax liability, cost recovery, gain on sale, and pre-tax cash flow

> 2. Differentiate between an income property and a non-income property in terms of measuring investment performance and property type

Investment Analysis of Non-income Property

> 1. Perform an investment analysis of a residential property's gain (or loss), taking into accounts its beginning basis, appreciation, capital improvements and ending basis

Investment Analysis of Income Property

> 1. Identify an income property's net operating income, tax liability, and pre-tax cash flow

> 2. Derive the property's tax liability and its after-tax cash flow

Investment Performance Analysis

> 1. Summarize the essential mechanics and components (I, R, V) underlying investment return and the main types of investment return

> 2. Describe the formulas for deriving price, cap rate, or net income given two known variables

> 3 Derive return on investment, return on cash, and return on equity given a hypothetical income property

Unit 15: Essential Characteristics of Real Estate Investments

---

Unit 15: Essential Characteristics of Real Estate Investments – Learning Objectives

When the student has completed Unit 15, he or she will be able to:

> **1. Summarize the salient characteristics of a real estate investment in terms of risk and return, and define the financial measurement components of taxable income, tax liability, cost recovery, gain on sale, and pre-tax cash flow**

> **2. Differentiate between an income property and a non-income property in terms of measuring investment performance and property type**

OVERVIEW OF REAL ESTATE INVESTMENTS

Any purchase of real estate constitutes the acquisition of an investment as opposed to incurring an expense. Similarly, any sale of real estate constitutes the disposition of an investment. In that regard, it behooves licensees to understand the essential principles and dynamics at play within an investment, and, more specifically, a real property investment.

Taken as a whole, people make investments in order to do something with excess monies that will either be a way to make a profit or to realize appreciation or the benefits of a tax shelter. Real estate investing is no different. Real estate potentially offers excellent investment benefits like all other investments. In addition, all investments involve varying degrees of risk – all of which works to define how much profit, appreciation or tax shelter you will enjoy -- if any. Again, real estate investments are no different. They have their own unique set of risks that investors must assume when they engage in real property investment activity.

This unit will present the basics of real estate investments – what they are, how they are analyzed and evaluated, and what measures of return are used to gauge an investment's relative value.

Income v non-income property. For the novice's understanding, real estate investments can be divided into two general areas: *income* property investments and *non-income* property investments. The former largely consists of commercial properties where investors are looking for rent, income, and profits. These investments include office, retail and industrial properties, as well as apartment buildings. The non-income property investment group consists primarily of unimproved land and owner-occupied residences where investors are looking for appreciation. In this unit, we will focus on defining, analyzing, and measuring the returns of both income and non-income investment properties.

INVESTMENT ESSENTIALS

Risk versus return

The general rule in investments is that the safer the investment, the more slowly it gains in value. The more you want it to gain, and the more quickly, the more you must risk losing it. How much do you want to earn, and how much are you willing to risk to earn it? Reward in investing corresponds directly to the degree of risk. If the investment is very safe, the return will be less. If the return is above average, there will be more risk of potential loss.

Management

Another aspect of investment is the amount of attention you must pay to it to make it work. You can deposit cash in a passbook account and forget about it. You can use your cash to buy a business and then run the business yourself to make your asset grow and earn. How much do you want to be involved in managing your investment?

Liquidity

The issue of exchangeability is an important one in investment. How easy is it to recover your invested resource, without loss, and exchange it for another one that you want? If there is a market for the type of resource you have¬- other people want to buy and sell it for themselves-- your investment is liquid. The most liquid form of financial investment is generally cash, since cash is itself a medium of exchange and people always want it. A more illiquid investment is one which takes a long time to exchange for something you prefer to own. How long are you willing to wait to recover your invested resource and its earnings?

REAL ESTATE AS AN INVESTMENT

Risks in real estate investing

Capital put into real estate is always subject to the full range of risk factors: market changes, income shortfalls, negative leverage, tax law changes, and poor overall return.

Demand uncertainty. Market demand for a specific type of property can decline. For example, a business district's retailers may vacate stores in an area in order to obtain better space in a new shopping center. Market downturns leave the income property investor with an unmarketable property or one which can only be re-leased at a loss of some portion of the original investment. Thus the expected reward from income or appreciation may never be obtained.

Development costs. Another risk of the investment property is the cost of development or operation. If start-up costs or ongoing operating costs exceed rental income, the owner must dip into additional capital resources to maintain the investment until its income increases. If income does not rise, or if costs do not decline, the investor can simply run out of money.

Negative leverage. Leverage is a constant risk in real estate investment. If the property fails to generate sufficient revenue, the costs of borrowed money can bankrupt the owner, just as development and operating costs can. Investors often overlook the fact that leverage only works when the yield on the investment exceeds the costs of borrowed funds.

Tax law changes. Tax law is an ongoing risk in long-term real estate investment. If the investor's tax circumstances change, or if the tax laws do, the investor may end up paying more capital gains and income taxes than planned, undermining the return on the investment. An investor needs to consider carefully the value of such potential tax benefits as deductions for mortgage interest, tax losses, deferred gains, exemptions, and tax credits for certain types of real estate investment.

Opportunity cost. Another consideration is opportunity cost. Opportunity cost is the return that an investor could earn on capital invested with minimal risk. If the real estate investment, with all its attendant risk, cannot yield a greater return than an investment elsewhere involving less risk, then the opportunity cost is too high for the real estate investment. Despite all the risks, real estate remains a popular investment, because, historically, the rewards have outweighed the risks. Real estate has proven to be relatively resistant to adverse inflationary trends that have hurt money, debt, and stock investments. In addition, real estate has proven to be a viable investment in view of the economy's continued expansion over the last fifty years.

Illiquidity of real estate

Compared with other classes of investment, real estate is relatively illiquid. Even in the case of liquidating a single-family residence, one can expect a marketing period of at least several months in most markets. In addition, it takes time for the buyer to obtain financing and to complete all the other phases of closing the transaction. Commercial and investment properties can take much longer, depending on market conditions, leases, construction, permitting, and a host of other factors. The investor who is in a hurry to dispose of such an investment can expect to receive a lower sales price than may be ideal. Compare this with the ease of drawing money out of a bank account or selling a stock.

Management intensive

Real estate tends to require a high degree of investor involvement in management of the investment. Even raw land requires some degree of maintenance to preserve its value: drainage, fencing, payment of taxes, and periodic inspection, to name a few tasks. Improved properties often require extensive management, including repairs, maintenance, onsite leasing, tenant relations, security, and fiscal management.

KEY INVESTMENT COMPONENTS

The key components of a non-income property are capital gain and appreciation. Capital gain (or loss) is the difference between what you paid for an investment and what you received when you sold it. Simply, the equation is ($ received minus $ paid). Appreciation gain or loss is purely a market increase or decrease in the property's value without respect to what was paid, added, depreciated, or received.

The key components of an income property investment are income, expenses, net income, depreciation, debt service and cash flow. In essence, on an annual basis, money in minus money out. Here is a closer look.

Taxable Income

Taxable income from investment real estate is the gross income received minus any expenses, deductions or exclusions that current tax law allows. Taxable income from real estate is added to the investor's other income and taxed at the investor's marginal tax rate. The following "Investment Analysis of an Income Property" section gives quantitative details.

Cost recovery or depreciation

Cost recovery, or depreciation, allows the owner of income property *to deduct a portion of the property's value from gross income each year over the life of the asset*. The "life of the asset" and the deductible portion are defined by law. In theory, the owner recovers the full cost of the investment if it is held to the end of the asset's economic life as defined by the Internal Revenue Service. At the time of selling the asset, the accumulated cost recovery is subtracted from the investment's original value as part of determining the taxable capital gain.

Cost recovery is allowed only for income properties and that portion of a non-income property which is used to produce income. It applies only to improvements. Land cannot be depreciated. The part of a property which can be depreciated is called the **depreciable basis**.

Depreciation schedules. Residential rental properties are depreciated over a period of 27.5 years. The basic annual deduction for such property is 3.636%, with adjustments for the month of the taxable year in which the property was placed in service. Non-residential income properties placed in service after 1994 are depreciated over a period of 39 years (basic annual percentage is 2.564%). The proper method of depreciation should be determined in consultation with a qualified tax advisor.

Gain on sale

When real estate, whether non-income or income, is sold, a taxable event occurs. If the sale proceeds exceed the original cost of the investment, subject to some adjustments, there is a capital gain that is subject to tax. If the sales proceeds are less than the original cost with adjustments, there is a capital loss.

Interest

Mortgage interest incurred by loans to buy, build, or materially improve a primary or secondary residence is deductible from gross income. The interest on a home equity loan may be deducted only if the loan is used to "buy, build or substantially improve" the home that secures the loan. Principal payments on a loan are not deductible.

For income properties that are held as investments, interest on debts incurred to finance the investment is deductible as investment interest up to the amount of net income received from the property.

In the following units, we will analyze a non-income property investment, an income-property investment, and how these investments are measured by investors to evaluate how worthwhile an investment is given its price and net yield.

SNAPSHOT REVIEW:

Unit 15: ESSENTIAL CHARACTERISTICS OF REAL ESTATE INVESTMENTS

OVERVIEW OF REAL ESTATE INVESTMENTS

- **Income v non-income property.** Income-producing property generates rent, net income, profits; non-income property largely consists of unimproved land and owner-occupied residences. These are held for appreciation

INVESTMENT ESSENTIALS

Risk versus return

- safer investments grow more slowly in value but with less volatility and insecurity

Management intensiveness

- real estate investment demands comparatively large amounts of time to manage

Liquidity

- a measure of how fast and easy it is to sell and recapture invested capital without loss

REAL ESTATE AS AN INVESTMENT

Risks in real estate investing

- **Demand uncertainty.** Market demand for specific type of property can decline or increase

- **Development costs.** Cost of development or operation can jeopardize desired returns

- **Negative leverage.** If property fails to generate sufficient revenue, costs of borrowed money can bankrupt owner, just as development and operating costs can

- **Tax law changes.** If investor's tax circumstances change, or tax laws do, investor may end up paying more capital gains and income taxes

- **Opportunity cost.** Return that investor could earn on capital invested elsewhere

- **Illiquidity of real estate.** Real estate is illiquid and takes longer to cash out

Management intensive

- high degree of investor involvement in management of investment

KEY INVESTMENT COMPONENTS

- non-income property-capital gain and appreciation

- income property- income, expenses, net income, depreciation, debt service, cash flow

Taxable income

- gross income received minus any expenses, deductions or exclusions that current tax law allows

Cost recovery or depreciation

- allows owner of income property to deduct portion of property's value from gross income each year over life of asset

- **Depreciation schedules.** Residential rental properties are depreciated over a period of 27.5 years

Gain on sale

- if sale proceeds exceed original cost of investment, subject to some adjustments, there is capital gain that is subject to tax

Interest

- mortgage interest deductible from gross income

==

Check Your Understanding Quiz:

Unit 15: Essential Characteristics of Real Estate Investments

Carefully read each question and provide your best answer based on what you learned in this module. Then check your answers against the Answer Key which immediately follows the quiz questions.

1. The return an investor could earn on capital invested elsewhere is referred to as which of the following?

   a. Capital gains
   b. Short-term growth
   c. Opportunity cost
   d. Accumulation

2. Elias bought an investment property for $250,000 and netted $300,000 upon its sale. What is his capital gain?

   a. $25,000
   b. <$50,000> loss
   c. $50,000
   d. 150%

3. What accounting practice allows the owner of an income property to deduct a portion of the property's value from gross income each year over the life of the asset?

   a. Taxable income
   b. Deduction
   c. Value loss
   d. Depreciation

4. An office investment property can be distinguished as a(n) _____.

   a. growth property.
   b. income property.
   c. retail property.
   d. non-income property.

5. Residential rental properties are depreciated over a period of time. What portion of the property is depreciable?

   a. The improvements
   b. The land
   c. The land and improvements
   d. These properties are not depreciable.

Exercise Workshop -- Unit 15: Essential Characteristics of Real Estate Investment

Exercise 15-1. Characteristics of Real Estate Investment

Synopsis:

In this exercise, the student will demonstrate their understanding of the terminology used in real estate investment.

Instructions:

Fill in the blank with an appropriate term describing some of the essential characteristics of real estate investment.

Exercise:

1. Consists of commercial properties where investors are looking for rent, income and profits: _____.

2. _____ consists primarily of unimproved land and owner-occupied residences.

3. One of the major disadvantages of investing in real estate is that it is relatively _____ due to the fact it takes time to sell it.

4. If the costs to borrow money on a piece of investment property exceed the return on investment received the investment is considered to be experiencing _____.

5. Real estate tends to require a high degree of investor involvement in the _____ of investment property.

6. _____ is a specific amount of an investment property's basis that can be deducted each year from gross income over the life of the asset.

7. The IRS allows income property to be depreciated over _____ years.

8. _____ from investment real estate is the gross income received minus operating expenses incurred, depreciation, and interest.

9. _____ is the return that an investor could otherwise earn on capital invested with minimal risk.

Unit 16: Investment Analysis of Non-income Property

Unit 16: Investment Analysis of Non-income Property – Learning Objectives

When the student has completed Unit 16, he or she will be able to:

1. Perform an investment analysis of a residential property's gain (or loss), taking into account its beginning basis, appreciation, capital improvements and ending basis

---

Investment analysis examines the economic performance of an investment. With a non-income property, the analysis examines and quantifies appreciation and capital gain and tax benefits.

A property acquired and used as a primary residence is an example of a non-income property. If a portion of a residence is used for business (i.e., a home office), this portion only may be treated as an income property for tax purposes. Since, by definition, a non-income property does not generate income, its value as an investment must come from one or more of the other sources: appreciation, leverage, or tax benefits. In the current context, we will limit our coverage to appreciation and capital gain.

Appreciation

Appreciation is the increase in value of an asset over time, usually stated as annual appreciation. A simple way to estimate appreciation on a primary residence is to subtract the price originally paid from the estimated current market value:

Current value - original price = total appreciation

For example, if a house was bought for $300,000 and its current estimated market value is $400,000, it has appreciated by $100,000.

Original price: $300,000

Current market value: $400,000

Total appreciation: $100,000

Total appreciation. Total appreciation can be stated as a *percentage increase* over the original price by dividing the estimated total appreciation by the original price.

The house in the last example has appreciated by 33%:

((Total appreciation)) ÷ (Original price) = % appreciated

100,000 ÷ 300,000=33%

Annual appreciation. To estimate the percentage of annual appreciation, divide the percent appreciated by the number of years the house has been owned:

$$(\% \text{ total appreciation}) \div (\text{years owned}) = \% \text{ appreciation per year}$$

If the house in the previous example has been owned for three years, the annual appreciation has been 11% per year.

$$(33\%) \div (3 \text{ years}) = 11\% \text{ appreciation per year}$$

Deductibles

The primary tax benefit available to the owner of a non-income property is the annual deduction for mortgage interest. The portion of annual mortgage payments that goes to repay principal must be subtracted to determine the amount paid for interest. Principal repayment is not deductible. Furthermore, depreciation is not allowed for non-income properties.

Tax liability

The seller of a principal residence may owe tax on capital gain that results from the sale. The IRS defines gain on the sale of a home **as amount realized from the sale minus the adjusted basis of the home sold.**

Amount realized. The amount realized, also known as net proceeds from sale, is expressed by the formula:

sale price - costs of sale = amount realized

The sale price is the total amount the seller receives for the home. This includes money, notes, mortgages or other debts the buyer assumes as part of the sale.

Costs of sale include brokerage commissions, relevant advertising, legal fees, seller-paid points and other closing costs. Certain fixing-up expenses, as discussed further below, can be deducted from the amount realized to derive an adjusted sale price for the purpose of postponing taxation on gain.

For example, Larry and Mary sold their home for $350,000. Their selling costs, including the commission they paid Broker Betty and amounts paid to inspectors, a surveyor, and the title company, amounted to ten percent of the selling price, or $35,000. The amount they realized from the sale was therefore $315,000.

Adjusted basis. Basis is a measurement of how much is invested in the property for tax purposes. Assuming that the property was acquired through purchase, the beginning basis is the cost of acquiring the property. Costs include cash and debt obligations, and such other settlement costs as legal and recording fees, abstract fees, surveys, charges for installing utilities, transfer taxes, title insurance, and any other amounts the buyer pays for the seller. These costs, if permitted by law, are added to the beginning basis.

The beginning basis is further *increased* by capital expenditures made while the property is owned. Additionally, the basis is *decreased* by depreciation, such as a periodic home office deduction.

Assessments paid for local improvements such as roads and sidewalks increase the property's basis. Other examples of capital improvements are: putting on a room addition, paving a gravel driveway, replacing a roof, adding central air conditioning, and rewiring the home. Expenditures not allowed to be added to basis include re-painting the house, fixing appliances, or repairing a window seal.

The basic formula for adjusted basis is:

Beginning basis

+ capital improvements

- exclusions, credits, depreciation

= adjusted basis

For example, Mary and Larry originally paid $200,000 for their home. They spent an additional $10,000 on a new central heating and cooling unit. Their adjusted basis at the time of selling it is therefore $210,000.

Gain on sale. The gain on sale of a primary residence is represented by the basic formula:

amount realized (net sales proceeds)

- adjusted basis

= gain on sale

Gain on sale, if it does not qualify for an exclusion under current tax law, is taxable.

Gain on Sale

Selling price of old home	$350,000
- Selling costs	35,000
= Amount realized	315,000
Beginning basis of old home	200,000
+ Capital improvements	10,000
= Adjusted basis of old home	210,000
Amount realized	315,000

- Adjusted basis	**210,000**
= Gain on sale	**105,000**

In the case of Mary and Larry, their capital gain was $315,000 - $210,000, or $105,000. They will owe tax on this amount in the year of the sale unless they qualify for the gains tax exclusion described as follows.

Gains tax exclusion

Current tax law provides for an exclusion of $250,000 for an individual taxpayer and $500,000 for married taxpayers filing jointly. The exclusion of gain from sale of a residence can be claimed every two years, provided the taxpayer

- owned the property for at least two years during the five years preceding the date of sale;
- used the property as principal residence for a total of two years during that five-year period;
- has waited two years since the last use of the exclusion for any sale.

Losses are not deductible, and there is no carry-over of any unused portion of the exclusion. Postponed gains from a previous home sale under the earlier rollover rules reduce the basis of the current home if that home was a qualifying replacement home under the old rule

SNAPSHOT REVIEW:

Unit 16: INVESTMENT ANALYSIS OF NON-INCOME PROPERTY

INVESTMENT ANALYSIS OF NON-INCOME PROPERTY

Appreciation

- increase in value of asset over time, stated as annual appreciation

- **Total appreciation.** Percentage increase over original price; dividing estimated total appreciation by original price

- **Annual appreciation.** Divide percent appreciated by number of years house has been owned

Deductibles

- mortgage interest

Tax liability

- seller of principal residence may owe tax on capital gain

- **Amount realized.** Net proceeds from sale

- **Adjusted basis.** Basis + capital improvements – depreciation, credits

- **Gain on sale.** Amount realized – adjusted basis

Gains tax exclusion

- $250,000 for individual taxpayer; $500,000 for married taxpayers filing jointly

===

Check Your Understanding Quiz:

Unit 16: Investment Analysis of Non-income Property

Carefully read each question and provide your best answer based on what you learned in this module. Then check your answers against the Answer Key which immediately follows the quiz questions.

1. Which of the following is the formula for the net proceeds from a sale?

   a. Amount realized + costs of sale
   b. Costs of sale / amount realized
   c. Sale price – costs of sale
   d. Amount realized – sale price

2. What is the term for the increase in value of an asset over time?

   a. Capital gains
   b. Appreciation
   c. Growth
   d. Total gains

3. The measurement of how much is invested in a property for tax purposes is called _____.

   a. depreciation.
   b. tax liability.
   c. accumulation.
   d. adjusted basis.

4. Which of the following is the formula for calculating adjusted basis?

   a. Beginning basis + capital improvements - exclusions
   b. Basis – capital improvements
   c. Amount realized + gain on sale
   d. Selling price – selling costs

5. The exclusion of gain from sale of a residence can be claimed every _____.

   a. 1 year.
   b. six months.
   c. two years.
   d. 7 months.

===

==

Exercise Workshop -- Unit 16: Investment Analysis of Non-Income Property

Exercise 16-1. Investment Analysis of Non-Income Property

Synopsis:

In this exercise, the student will calculate the capital gain or loss on a piece of property.

Instructions:

Solve the problems below for the indicated value of the described properties.

Exercises:

Brenda and Tom bought their home ten years ago for $350,000. During the time they owned the house, they added a pool worth $25,000 and a screened porch worth $10,000. They incurred a total of $3,660 in closing costs in the initial sale. They recently sold their home for $714,000 and incurred closing costs of $1,725.

1. Calculate the appreciated value of their home.

2. Calculate the adjusted basis of their home.

3. Calculate the amount realized.

4. Calculate the capital gain or loss on the sale of their home.

5. How much will they pay in taxes?

Olivia and Nicholas bought their home seven years ago for $250,000 with closing costs of $3,200. During the time of their ownership, they installed a new A/C system worth $12,500. They recently sold their home for $260,500 and had selling expenses of $3,500

6. Calculate the appreciated value of their home.

7. Calculate the adjusted basis of their home.

8. Calculate the amount realized.

9. Calculate the capital gain or loss on the sale of their home.

Unit 17: Investment Analysis of Income Property

Unit 17: Investment Analysis of Income Property – Learning Objectives

When the student has completed Unit 17, he or she will be able to:

> **1. Identify an income property's net operating income, tax liability, and pre-tax cash flow**
>
> **2. Derive the property's tax liability and its after-tax cash flow**

Overview

Income properties are those which are held primarily for the generation of income, return, and tax benefits. In addition to commercial and investment properties such as office buildings and stores, income properties include residential rental properties such as apartment complexes and single-family houses rented out to tenants.

An important difference between income and non-income properties is that deductions for depreciation are allowed on income properties. Income properties, like non-income properties, generate a gain (or loss) on sale, and they also create an annual income stream. The annual income streams are determined on both a pre-tax and after-tax basis in order to determine the productivity of the investment. In this unit we will examine how the income stream is identified and calculated. In the next unit, we will bring in the various measures of investment performance that enable investors to calibrate how well their investments are faring.

Pre-tax cash flow

Cash flow. Cash flow is the difference between the amount of actual cash flowing into the investment as revenue, and out of the investment for expenses, debt service, and all other items. Cash flow takes into account cash items only, and therefore excludes depreciation, which is not a cash expense.

Pre-tax cash flow, or cash flow before taxation, is calculated as follows:

	Pre-tax cash flow
	potential rental income
-	**vacancy and collection loss**
=	**effective rental income**
+	**other income**
=	**gross operating income (GOI)**
-	**operating expenses**
-	**reserves**
=	**net operating income (NOI)**

-	debt service (principal and interest)	
=	pre-tax cash flow	

Potential rental income is the annual amount that would be realized if the property is fully leased or rented at the scheduled rate. Vacancy and collection loss is rental income lost due to vacancies or tenants' failure to pay rent.

Effective rental income is the potential income adjusted for these losses where vacancy – or estimated vacancy – is subtracted out.

Other income is any other income the property generates, such as from laundry or parking charges. When other income is added to effective rental income, the result is the investment's "top line", or **gross operating income**.

Operating expenses paid by the landlord include such items as utilities, repairs and maintenance. These outflows are deducted from gross operating income.

Reserves. Some owners also set aside a cash reserve each year to build up a fund for capital replacements in the future, for example, to replace a roof or a furnace. *Cash reserves are not deductible for tax purposes until spent as deductible repairs or maintenance*. Note also that reserves are not necessary in deriving an investment's performance. If they are not spent, they simply amount to taxable income to the investor.

Net operating expenses. The remainder of gross operating income minus expenses and reserve allowances is **net operating income** (NOI). Generally, NOI is the number used to derive an investment's pre-tax return and is therefore a key figure to identify in investment analysis.

Debt service. When the annual amounts paid for debt service, *including principal and interest*, is subtracted from net operating income, the remainder is the investment's **pre-tax cash flow**. Ultimately, pre-tax cash flow is how much cash came into the investment minus how much cash went out – before accounting for taxes.

For instance, a consider that a small office building of 3,500 square feet rents at $20 per square foot per year. If fully rented, the annual rental income would be $70,000. Historically, we'll assume, the property averages $4,200 in vacancy and collection losses. Equipment rental will provide an additional $2,000 per year in income. The owner will have to pay operating expenses amounting to ten dollars per square foot, or $35,000 per year. The owner sets aside one dollar per square foot, or $3,500 per year, for reserves. The owner financed the purchase of the building with a loan that requires annual debt service in the amount of $20,000. The pre-tax cash flow for the building is illustrated in the following exhibit.

Pre-tax Cash Flow Illustration

	potential rental income	**$70,000**
-	**vacancy and collection loss**	**4,200**
=	**effective rental income**	**65,800**

+	other income	2,000
=	gross operating income	67,800
-	operating expenses	35,000
-	reserves	3,500
=	net operating income (NOI)	29,300
-	debt service	20,000
=	pre-tax cash flow	$9,300

Tax liability

The owner's tax liability on income from the property is based on *taxable income rather than cash flow*. To get to taxable income from pre-tax cash flow requires accounting for reserves, depreciation, and interest paid on the loan.

Taxable income. Taxable income and tax liability are derived from NOI as follows:

<u>Tax Liability</u>

net operating income (NOI)

+	reserves
-	interest expense
-	cost recovery expense
=	taxable income
x	tax rate
=	tax liability

Taxable income is net operating income minus all additional allowable deductions plus the amount allocated for reserves (since those unspent amounts are not taxable).

Depreciation, reserves and loan interest. **Cost recovery expense, or depreciation** is allowed as a deduction from income for tax purposes, while allowances for **reserves** and payments on loan principal payback are not allowed as tax deductions. Thus, since reserves were deducted from gross operating income to determine NOI, this amount *must be added back in.* As only the interest portion of debt service is deductible, the principal amount must be removed from the debt service payments and the *interest expense deducted from NOI.* The remainder is **taxable income.** Taxable income is then *multiplied by the owner's marginal tax bracket*, to estimate the investment's **income tax liability**.

Note on tax rate: when a rental property is owned as an individual or by way of a pass-through entity (partnership, LLC treated as a partnership for tax purposes, or S corporation), its net income is taxed at the individual's personal marginal income tax rate. The next exhibit shows the tax liability for the previous example using an assumed individual rate of 24%.

Tax Liability Illustration

net operating income (NOI)		29,300
+	reserves	3,500
-	interest expense	10,000
-	cost recovery expense	22,000
=	taxable income	800
x	tax rate (24%)	
=	tax liability	192

In the example, $3,500 in reserves must be added back to net income. Then, $10,000 interest and $22,000 depreciation (non-cash) are deducted from (net income + reserves). (Note that principal payments on the loan are not deductible.) This calculation results in $800 taxable interest. At a 24% rate, the investor's tax liability is $192.

After-tax cash flow

After-tax cash flow is simply the amount of income from the property that actually goes into the owner's pocket after income tax is paid. It is figured as pre-tax cash flow minus taxes:

After-tax cash flow

Pre-tax cash flow	
-	tax liability
=	after-tax cash flow

The after-tax cash flow for the sample property is illustrated in the following exhibit.

After-tax Cash Flow Illustration

pre-tax cash flow		9,300
-	tax liability	192
=	after-tax cash flow	9,108

SNAPSHOT REVIEW:

Unit 17: INVESTMENT ANALYSIS OF INCOME PROPERTY

Overview

- income properties held for generation of income, return, and tax benefits

Pre-tax cash flow

- **Cash flow.** Difference between amount of cash flowing into investment as revenue, and out of investment for expenses, debt service, etc.

- **Pre-tax cash flow.** Income minus expenses minus debt service plus depreciation

- **Potential rental income.** Annual amount that would be realized if property is fully leased or rented at scheduled rate

- **Effective rental income.** Potential income adjusted for losses where vacancy/estimated vacancy is subtracted out

- **Other income.** Any other income property generates

- **Operating expenses.** Utilities, repairs and maintenance

- **Reserves.** Cash reserve each year to build up fund for capital replacements in future

- **Net operating expenses.** Gross operating income minus expenses and reserve allowances

- **Debt service.** Principal and interest payments

Tax liability

- **Taxable income.** Net operating income minus all additional allowable deductions (including depreciation) plus the amount allocated for reserves

- **Depreciation, reserves and loan interest.** Depreciation and interest allowed as deduction from income; allowances for reserves not allowed as tax deductions

After-tax cash flow

- pre-tax cash flow minus tax liability

==

Check Your Understanding Quiz:

Unit 17: Investment Analysis of Income Property

Carefully read each question and provide your best answer based on what you learned in this module. Then check your answers against the Answer Key which immediately follows the quiz questions.

1. Some owners set aside a _____ to build up a fund for capital replacements in the future.

   a. rainy day fund
   b. sinking fund
   c. debt service
   d. cash reserve

2. What is one of the most significant differences between income and non-income properties?

   a. Non-income properties have cash reserves.
   b. Income properties are held for income and net profit.
   c. Pre-tax cash flow is calculated for non-income properties.
   d. Deductions for appreciation are allowed on non-income properties.

3. Which of the following is the formula for net operating expenses?

   a. Gross operating income – expenses and reserve allowance
   b. Pre tax cash flow – expenses
   c. Adjusted basis + reserves
   d. Expenses – net income

4. Which of the following is included in debt service?

   a. Depreciation
   b. Reserves
   c. Principal and interest on the loan
   d. Commissions

5. What is another name for cost recovery expense?

   a. Depreciation
   b. Net Income
   c. Appreciation
   d. Income liability

==

Exercise Workshop -- Unit 17: Investment Analysis of Income Property

Exercise 17-1. Investment Analysis of Income Property

Synopsis:

In this exercise, the student will determine the after-tax cash flow for each of the following scenarios.

Exercise:

1. Joe recently bought a 25-unit apartment complex. The complex has 13 3-bedroom apartments that rent for $1,500 per month, eight 2-bedroom apartments that rent for $1000 per month, and four studio apartments that rent for $850 per month. Vacancy and collection losses for this area run about 5.5% of the potential gross income.

The property has vending machines and a coin operating laundry that brings in other income of $550 per month.

Operating expenses run approximately 10% of the Potential Gross Income for fixed expenses, 15% of the Effective Gross Income for variable expenses, and 5% of Effective Gross Income for Repairs and Replacements.

Interest payments on their mortgage come to $12,600 annually. The building allows for a cost recovery expense of $43,000 per year.

Currently, Joe's income tax rate is 22%. Calculate Joe's after-tax cash flow for this property.

2. Alex recently bought an 18-unit apartment complex. All of the units are two bedrooms, two bath units that rent for $950 per month. Vacancy and collection losses run approximately 7.5%, and there is no additional income.

Operating expenses run approximately 30% of the Effective Gross Income. Operating expenses include $5,000 per year for Reserves for Replacement.

The Annual Debt Service is $50,000, of which 30% is interest this year. Using Straight-line depreciation, the cost recovery rate for this year is $15,000.

Alex's current tax rate is 20%. Calculate Alex's after-tax cash flow for this property.

Unit 18: Investment Performance Analysis

Unit 18: Investment Performance Analysis – Learning Objectives

When the student has completed Unit 18, he or she will be able to:

1. Summarize the essential mechanics and components (I, R, V) underlying investment return and the main types of investment return

2. Describe the formulas for deriving price, rate of return, and net income given two known variables

3 Derive return on investment, return on cash, and return on equity given a hypothetical income property

Forms of investment return

There are numerous types of investment return, each of which tells investors how well an investment has performed in a given area of its financial results. Examples include cash-on-cash, return on equity, return on investment, payback period, and internal rate of return. For the present context, we will examine the most common return ratios used in investment analysis: return on investment; return on cash; and return on equity. Each form of return uses the same three components on an investment: it's income, its value or price, and its rate of return.

Income. The income component of an investment answers the question "how much money does the investment generate." This is derived by adding up total income and taking out all the relevant expenses.

More importantly, when considering whether to make an investment, a second question that must be answered is "how much money _should_ the investment generate, given its price and given the investor's required rate of return. The second question requires the investor to solve the basic return formula for income:

(Investor's required return X Value (or Price)) = Income; or (R x V) = I

Here, to justify the investment of a given amount of money and to meet the investor's required rate of return given all the risks, the investment must generate a specific amount of income.

Take, for example, a building priced at $3 million. The investor, who must generate a 15% pre-tax return on these types of properties, completes the formula (R x V) = I and realizes the property must generate $450,000 to be worth her trouble ($3MM x 15% = $450,000). The bottom line: if this property does in fact generate $450K or more, the investment is justified.

Value or price. The value, or price, component of an investment answers the question "what is the price or value of the investment?"

In the case where an investor is considering whether to make an investment, the related question that must be answered is "how much money _should_ the investment cost, given its income and given the investor's required rate of return. To answer this, we basically move the same I-R-V equation around to solve for Value:

Income ÷ Rate of return = Value or Price

Here, to justify an investment that generates a given amount of income and to meet the investor's required rate of return given all the risks, the investment must have a specific maximum price. Returning to our example, if we are considering a property that generates $300,000, and we require a minimum return of 10%, then the property must be priced at no more than $3 million. ($300,000 ÷ 10% or .10) = $3 million.)

Rate of return. The third component of investment performance is the investment's rate of return, or the percent of return, or yield rate. Expressed as a percent, this number answers the question, "what is my return on the investment given its price and investment performance.

Rate of return is perhaps the most important index of an investment's performance, since it ultimately tells an investor how much money he or she can make given the amount of money the investor has to invest.

To derive rate of return, we reconfigure the same equation into its third expression:

Income ÷ Price = Rate of return

Returning to the example, we can identify that the given $3,000,000 property which generates $450,000 has an investment return of 15 % ($450 K ÷ $3 million) = 15%.

Using these three equations enable investors to assess either what a property's price should be given its income and the investor's required return; what its income should be given a price and required return; and what its return is given its income and price. To review these equations, we have:

Income = Rate or return x Value or Price

Value or Price = Income ÷ Rate of return

Rate of Return = Income ÷ Value or Price

Investment performance analysis

There are three principal forms of investment returns used to evaluate investment properties. They are return on investment; cash-on-cash return, and return on equity. These are expressed in formulas as follows:

Return on investment:	**net operating income ÷ price = return on investment (ROI)**
Cash-on-cash return:	**cash flow ÷ cash invested = cash-on-cash return (C on C)**
Return on equity:	**net operating income ÷ equity = return on equity (ROE)**

Return on investment. This is the most primary measure of an investment's performance. As discussed, it compares the investment's net income to the price paid for the investment. From our previous analysis, this would be net operating income (NOI) divided by the total price paid for the property. Reviewing our illustration, we have:

Income ÷ Price = Rate of return

$450,000 ÷ 3,000,000 = 15%

Cash-on-cash return. If an investor wants to know his or her investment inclusive of financing, the investor must use the C on C performance measure. As shown, this is expressed as cash flow divided by cash invested. For example if our illustration example had a million dollar loan for underlying financing, and its debt service was $50,000, its C on C return would be:

($450,000 – 50,000), or $400,000 cash flow ÷ $2 million cash invested = 20%

Return on equity. Many investors want to know the return on their total stake in an investment which can include not only the initial cash invested, but the accumulated depreciation, equity build-up, and appreciation of the investment as expressed by its current market value.

The formula for equity is market value (or accumulated book value) minus total current debt principal. In our example, let's assume all factors reducing the property's equity totals $800,000 (1 million loan minus some principal paydown plus nominal appreciation minus accumulated depreciation). The current market value is estimated to be $3,000,000. Thus, the investor's current equity is $2.2 million (3 million – 800,000). From the original example, net operating income is posited at $450,000.

Therefore, the property's return on equity is:

return on equity (ROE) = (net operating income ÷ equity)

$450,000 Net income ÷ 2.2 million equity = 20.4%

Note also that some investors prefer to use cash flow to derive ROE. This would change the formula to be (cash flow ÷ equity) instead of (net income ÷ equity).

SNAPSHOT REVIEW:

Unit 18: INVESTMENT PERFORMANCE ANALYSIS

Forms of investment return

- **Income.** Adding up total income and taking out all relevant expenses

- **Value or price.** Income divided by rate of return

- **Rate of return.** Percent of return, or yield rate; income divided by price

Investment performance analysis

- **Return on investment.** Measure of an investment's performance

- **Cash-on-cash return.** Cash flow divided by cash invested

- **Return on equity.** Net operating income divided by equity

Check Your Understanding Quiz:

Unit 18: Investment Performance Analysis

Carefully read each question and provide your best answer based on what you learned in this module. Then check your answers against the Answer Key which immediately follows the quiz questions.

1. Which of the following is the correct formula for rate of return?

    a. Cash flow / cash invested
    b. Income / price
    c. gross operating income / price
    d. Price - income

2. The three principal forms of investment returns used to evaluate investment properties are return on investment, return on equity, and _____.

    a. cash-on-cash return.
    b. operating income.
    c. cash flow.
    d. value income.

3. Alice is an investor who knows she wants to generate a certain amount of income with a specific rate of return. How can she use this information to calculate the price she should offer?

    a. Alice should divide the rate of return by the income.
    b. She should multiply the rate of return by the income.
    c. She should divide the income by the rate of return.
    d. She should add the income to the rate of return.

4. Which of the following is the most primary measure of an investment's performance?

    a. Cash-on-cash return
    b. Return on investment
    c. Return on equity
    d. Value return

5. The formula for a property's return on equity is _____.

    a. income / price.
    b. cash flow / cash invested.
    c. price x income.
    d. net operating income / equity.

Exercise Workshop -- Unit 18: Investment Performance Analysis

Exercise 18-1. Investment Performance Analysis

Synopsis:

In this exercise, the student will learn how to evaluate an investment to determine if it meets the objectives of their investor client.

Instructions:

Solve each of the following questions using the information given in the problem.

Exercises:

1. An investor is looking at buying a property listed for $2 million. The property has a history of generating a Net Operating Income of $150,000, and the investor wants at least a 9% return on investment. Should the investor buy this piece of property?

2. What would be the return on investment if a piece of property sells for $3 million and generates $450,000 per year in cash flow?

3. How much would a buyer be willing to pay for a piece of property that has an overall capitalization rate of 7% and generates annual cash revenue of $250,000?

4. What would the cash-on-cash return be on a piece of property with a cash flow of $550,000 and an initial investment of $5.6 million?

5. Using the information from Unit 17, Problem 1, what is the approximate value of the property considering a 10% overall capitalization rate?

Exercise Workshops – Answer Key

Exercise 1.1 Answers:

1.   A R & U – This describes a single agency relationship. The Broker should have Lou and Mary sign a Listing Agreement and give them a copy of the South Carolina Disclosure of Real Estate Brokerage Relationships form.

2.   D, R, S, & U – This describes a designated agency relationship. The brokerage will be a dual agency, but with the Broker assigning the buyer and seller to separate agents within her brokerage, she has created a designated agency relationship. The sellers should sign a Listing Agreement, and the buyer should sign a Buyers Brokerage Agreement. Both parties should be given a copy of the South Carolina Disclosure of Real Estate Brokerage Relationship form.

3.   B, R, S, & U - This describes a dual agency relationship. Broker Leslie should have a listing agreement with the seller and a buyer's brokerage agreement signed by the buyer. Both parties should be given a copy of the South Carolina Disclosure of Real Estate Brokerage Relationship form.

4.   C, T, & U – This describes a transaction brokerage relationship. In this relationship, there are no fiduciary requirements on the Broker. The Broker is just assisting his customer in completing the sales and purchase contract. Broker John should give Bob a Transaction Broker disclosure along with the South Carolina Disclosure of Real Estate relationship form.

Exercise 2.1 Answers:

Agent Ron should ensure that the following items are disclosed on this piece of property:

- Lead-based paint disclosure because the home was built before 1978
- Radon gas
- Roof repaired using a patch
- The bathroom ceiling needs repair due to water damage
- Mildew or mold in basement
- No venting in the basement – high risk of carbon monoxide
- Septic system
- Water well

Agent Ron should ensure all parts of the Property Disclosure Form are completed. He should ask questions on any additional issues that appear on the disclosure.

He does not need to disclose the property as stigmatized because of the double homicide that occurred onsite or that a sex offender lives around the corner.

See attached copy of the South Carolina mandatory form for property condition disclosure. A copy of the form may be downloaded from

https://llr.sc.gov/re/recpdf/Property-Condition-Disclosure-Statement-06.01.2023.pdf

Exercise 4.1 Answers:

1. Voidable Contract. Robbie is only 17-year-old and thus is not competent to sign the contract. He must have a parent co-sign for him. He may cancel the contract at any time and would not be held responsible for breach of contract.

2. Valid Contract. All of the contract validity requirements are present in this case.

3. Unenforceable Contract. John does not own the home and does not have his father's permission to sell the house. The contract is missing a voluntary act of good faith by the owner.

4. Unenforceable Contract. The contract is not for a legal purpose. Selling a cannabis farm is not legal in the state of South Carolina.

5. Voidable Contract. All real estate contracts consider time is of the essence, which means that all dates must be upheld and met, or the agreement may be regarded as voidable or void. In this case, it would be up to Martha to extend the date to allow Max more time to submit the escrow deposit, or Martha may void the contract.

Exercise 4.2 Answers:

In this case, the judge ruled that Cindi and Tom were in breach of contract. However, he denied the developer's request for specific performance.

The judge did award liquidated damages for $20,000, the escrow deposit, and compensatory damages in the amount of $10,000 for the developer's upgrades to the condo.

Since Cindi was a licensed real estate agent and wrote up the contract but did not include financing information, the judge ordered that Cindi and Tom pay an additional $15,000 in punitive damages. The judge stated that Cindi should have known to put in a financing clause, keeping them out of court.

Exercise 5.1 Answers:

Procuring cause is the person who starts the chain of events that lead to the sale of the property.

Chris is procuring cause in this particular case. Jay had planned on using Chris as his Realtor all along, and if Elizabeth had asked, he would have stated this. The courts have decided that merely showing the property or having an open house does not start the chain of events that lead to the sale of a house. It begins when negotiations begin or significant discussions about the house start.

Since Elizabeth would not speak to Jay about his intentions or even accompany him into the house to answer any questions, she did not start the chain of events leading to the sale of the property. Chris and his Broker are entitled to the entire buyer's side commission.

Exercise 5.2 Answers:

Exercise 1   Exercise 2

    1. C   1. E
    2. B   2. B
    3. D   3. C
    4. A   4. D
    5. E   5. A

Exercise 6.1 Answers:

    1. D
    2. B
    3. F
    4. A
    5. E
    6. H
    7. C
    8. G

Exercise 6.2 Solution: Purchase and Sale Contract for Residential Real Estate

PARTIES: _____ **Gloria & Stephen Grigsby (H.W)** _____ (Seller) and
_____ **Dawn & Mark Spencer (H/W)** _____ (Buyer)

Agree to sell and convey real and personal property as described below.

PROPERTY DESCRIPTION:

Street Address: __ **1436 Highland Road, Columbia, SC 29000** _____

Located in: __**Richland**_____ County, South Carolina. Tax ID: __**R1234-12-21**_____

Real Property: Legal Description: __ **Block 12, Lot C Richmond Height**
Subdivision_____

Personal Property: _____ **Refrigerator, Range, D/W, and all fixtures** _____

_____

Purchase Price:……………………………………………………………………….. $__ **175,000** ____

Escrow Deposit (X) accompanies offer or (_) due with ____ days ………………$_ **5,000** _____

Escrow Agent Information: Name __John's Title__

Address: __321 Anywhere Street, Columbia, SC__

Phone: __800-555-4321__   Email: __JTitle@gmail.com__

Financing: Express as dollar amount or percentage $ __150,000__

(X) Conventional (_) FHA (_) VA (_) Owner Financing   APR% __4% max__

Cash to Close $ __$20,000__

Time to Accept Offer and Count-Offer: __06/13/2022__

Closing Date: __On or before 08/01/2022__

ADDENDA ADDED: __HOA Disclosure, Lead Paint, Appraisal__

ADDITIONAL TERMS:
__N/A__

_____

_____   _____

Buyer's Signature   Seller's Signature

Exercise 9.1 Answers:

1. A
2. A
3. A
4. A
5. C
6. B
7. B
8. A
9. B
10. B

Exercise 11.1 Answers:

1. C & F. In this case, as long as it is the first offense, the commission would probably order the agent's license to be suspended and that the agent takes a class in Escrow Fund Management. If this agent has appeared before the commission before, they will revoke this agent's license.

2. D. Since this case involved arson in an insurance case, the commission would probably revoke the agent's real estate license. Arson is considered a violent crime, and the case is related to the real estate industry because it was in conjunction with insurance fraud. The commission would probably see this person as a threat to the public.

3. A, B, & F. This offense probably occurred due to a lack of knowledge from the agent. The commission would likely issue a fine and put the agent on probation. They would further order her to take an Escrow Management Class and sit in on two commission meetings. Any further violations would result in the revocation of her license.

4. D. The commission would probably revoke Mike's license. This cause meets the criteria for criminal fraud.

5. A, C, & F. The commission would suspend Jill's real estate license and order her to pay a fine. During her suspension, she would be ordered to retake the Broker's course to refamiliarize herself with laws surrounding disclosure.

Remember, these are just example cases. The commission takes each case individually and allows respondents to appeal their case. The answers above are based on guidelines given to the commission. These are not the only possible outcomes.

Exercise 12.1 Answers:

1. This scenario violates Title VIII of the 1968 Civil Rights Act, also known as the Fair Housing Act. Specifically, this is known as steering. The correct response from the agent would be to ask her client if there was a specific neighborhood she was interested in looking at property. The agent should not take her to a particular area due to her client's race or religion.

2. This scenario violates the Fair Housing Act as well as the Home Mortgage Disclosure Act. This practice is known as redlining. To give out a "conforming loan," banks have set criteria the property and the mortgagor must meet. If they meet the qualifications, the bank must give the loan. Not giving a loan because of the socio-economic make-up of the community or the area's crime rate is a violation of the laws.

3. This scenario violates Fair Housing Act and the Americans with Disabilities Act. A landlord cannot charge more rent or a higher deposit to someone with a Disability. If a tenant asks for reasonable accommodations, the landlord must allow the tenant to modify the property at their own expense and agree to return the property to its original condition when they move out.

4. This scenario is a violation of the Clayton/Sherman Anti-trust Act. Specifically, it describes price-fixing—the group is working together to fix the prices within a specific area to make more money.

5. This scenario is a violation of the Fair Housing Act and the 1866 Civil Rights Act. Just by asking the question about the buyer's race, the seller is guilty. The agent is equally culpable for answering the question. Her response should have been, "it is irrelevant." The Department of Justice has been fining agents $1,000 in cases where they answered the question, even if they did not violate the law any further.

Exercise 12.2 Answers:

1.   Pathway to Professionalism
2.   The Public, the Property, & Peers
3.   1913
4.   C2EX – Commitment to Excellence
5.   To act with integrity & honesty
6.   Articles 1 & 2 (honesty and transparency)
7.   Article 10

Exercise 13.1 Answers:

1.   NW ¼ of the NE ¼ of the SW ¼ of Section 13, Tier 3 North, Range 4 West

SW ¼ of Section 13 = (¼ x 640 acres) or 160 acres

NE ¼ of SW ¼ = (1/4 x 160 acres) or 40 acres

NW ¼ of NE ¼ = (¼ x 40 acres) or 10 acres

Shortcut answer: multiply all fractions times 640 acres (¼ x ¼ x ¼) x 640 acres = 10 acres

2.   NE ½ of the NE ¼ of the SE ¼ of Section 2, T5N, R6W

(½ x ¼ x ¼) x 640 acres = (1/32 x 64) = 2 acres

(43,560 SF/acre x 2) = 8,710 SF.

3. A piece of land is rectangular in shape. The lot is 250 ft x 500 ft. What is the area of the lot?

Area = base x height

A = 250 x 500 = 125,000 SF

4. A piece of land is triangular in shape. The lot has a base of 300 feet and a height of 50 feet. What is the area of the lot?

Area = base x height/2

A = 300 x 50/2 = 7,500 SF

5. A piece of land is a trapezoid. The bases of the lot are 250 feet and 150 feet, with a height of 30 feet. What is the area of the lot?

$$\text{Area} = \text{height (base 1 + base 2)/2}$$

$$A = 30((250 + 150) \div 2) = 30\ (200) = 6{,}000\ SF$$

6.   What is the total square footage?

Living Room	15' x 16'	240 sq. ft.
Dining Room	10' x 10'	100 Sq. ft.
Kitchen	10' x 12'	120 sq. ft.
Bedroom #1	15' x 19'	285 sq. ft.
Bedroom #2	10' x 12'	120 sq. ft
Bedroom #3	10' x 10'	100 sq. ft.
Bedroom #4	10' x 11'	110 sq. ft.
Bathroom #1	8' x 5'	40 sq. ft.
Bathroom #2	5' x 5'	25 sq. ft.
Bathroom #3	5' x 5'	25 sq. ft.	Calculate living area
Front Porch	5' x 8'	40 sq. ft
Back Porch	10' X 15'	150 sq. ft.
Garage	20' x 25'	500 sq. ft.

Total Square Footage   1855 sq. ft.

Total Living Area   1165 sq. ft.

Exercise 14.1 Answers:

Sales Comparison Approach Illustration:

Adjustments

	Subject	Comp A	Comp B	Comp C	Comp D
Sales Price	???	$850,000	$900,000	$750,000	$800,000
Financing Terms	Standard	Standard	Standard	Standard	Standard
Sales Date	Now	Equal	Equal	Equal	Equal
Construction Quality	Good	Equal	-$50,000	equal	+$25,000
No. of Room	10	10	10	8	8
No. of BDRM	4	+$5,000	same	+$5,000	+$10,000
No. of Baths	3	-$3,000	same	+$3,000	+$3,000
Gross Living Area	2,500	2,200	2,600	2,100	1,900
Adjust for Living Area		+$2,000	-$2,000	+$2,000	+$2,000
Garage	2-car	Same	Same	Same	Same
Landscaping	Good	Equal	Equal	Equal	Equal
Net Adjustments		+$4,000	-$52,000	+$10,000	+$40,000
Value		$854,000	$848,000	$760,000	$840,000

Property should be listed between $760,000 to $850,000.

Exercise 15.1 Answers:

1. Income property

2. Non-Income property

3. Illiquid

4. Negative leverage

5. Management

6. Depreciation

7. 39

8. Taxable income

9. Opportunity cost

Exercise 16.1 Answers:

1. Current value – original price = total appreciation

    $714,000 - $350,000 = $364,000

2. Beginning basis – sells costs + capital improvements = adjusted basis

    $350,000 - $3,660 + $35,000 = $381,340

3. Current value – cost of sale = amount realized

    $714,000 - $1,725 = $712,275

4. Amount realized – Adjusted basis = gain/loss on sale

    $712,275 - $381,340 = $330,935 capital gain

5. Zero, the capital gain is below the $500,000 threshold for a married couple filing jointly. They are eligible for the exemption since it was their principal residence for more than two years.

6. Current value – original price = total appreciation

    $260,500 - $250,000 = -$10,500

7. Beginning basis – sells costs + capital improvements = adjusted basis

    $250,000 - $3,200 + $12,500 = $259,300

8. Current value – cost of sale = amount realized

    $260,500 - $3,500 = $257,000

9. Amount realized – adjusted basis = gain/loss on sale

    $257,000 - $259,300 = -$2,300 capital loss

Exercise 17.1 Answers:

1. Potential Gross Income: $370,800

        (4 x $850 x 12 mths) $40,800

        (13 x $1,500 x 12 mths) $234,000

        (8 x $1,000 x 12 mths) $96,000

    -   Vacancy & Collection :(5% of PGI) $18,540

+ Other Income: $ 6,600

        ($550 x 12 mths)

= Effective Gross Income: $358,860

    -   Operating Expenses: $108,852

        Fixed Expenses (10% PGI) $37,080

        Variable Expenses (15% EGI) $53,829

        Reserves for Replacements $17,943

= Net Operating Income: $250,008

+ Reserves for Replacements $ 5,000

- Debt Service Interest   (30% $50,000) $ 15,000

- Cost Recovery $ 15,000

= Pre-tax Cash Flow $225,008

- Tax Liability (22%) $ 49,502

=After Tax Cash Flow $175,506

2. Potential Gross Income: $205,200

        (18 x $950 x 12 mths) $205,200

- Vacancy & Collection : (7.5% of PGI) $15,390

+ Other Income: $ 00

= Effective Gross Income: $189,810

- Operating Expenses: (30% EGI) $ 56,943

= Net Operating Income: $132,867

+ Reserves for Replacements $ 5,000

- Debt Service Interest	$ 12,600
- Cost Recovery	$ 43,000
= **B**efore-tax Cash Flow	$ 82,267
- **T**ax Liability (20%)	$ 16,453
=**A**fter Tax Cash Flow	$65,814

Exercise 18.1 Answers:

1. Value = Net Operating Income/Return on Investment

   = $150,000/ 9% = $1,666,667

   The investor would want to pass on this piece of property because it will not give him the rate of return that he requires.

2. Return on Investment = Cash Flow / Value

   = $450,000/$3,000,000 = .15 or 15%

3. Value = Cash Flow/ Capitalization Rate

   = $250,000/ 7% = $3,571,429

4. Cash-on-Cash Return – Cash Flow/ Investment

   = $550,000/$5,600,000 = .098 or 9.8%

5. Value = Net Operating Income/Overall Capitalization Rate

   = 250,008/ 10% = $2,500,080

Answer Key for Quizzes

Unit 1: Agency

1. b. negotiated between broker and client.
2. a. sex offender information.
3. a. South Carolina Disclosure of Real Estate Brokerage Relationships form.
4. c. Transaction brokerage agreement
5. d. the property cannot be listed in the MLS.
6. a. 1978.
7. b. Mediation
8. d. Conveying marketable title to the property
9. b. The buyer
10. c. Designated Agency Agreement

Unit 2: Property Disclosure

1. a. Urea formaldehyde
2. b. Water Quality Act of 1987
3. c. Brownfields
4. b. Foreclosure sale
5. d. Radon
6. a. Murder that occurred on the property
7. b. Mold
8. c. EPA
9. a. environmental site assessment
10. b. carbon monoxide.

Unit 3: Other Brokerage Disclosures

1. a. Megan's Law
2. c. Stigmatized property
3. b. As-Is condition
4. c. On the first page of the contract
5. c. SORT
6. d. It is provided at no charge by the U.S. Department of Justice to the State of South Carolina.
7. a. Buyer's agents must advise buyers of their ability to determine the presence of registered offenders.
8. d. Chase must disclose his license status to all parties involved.
9. c. Subject property is occupied by an individual infected with HIV
10. a. Individual states

Unit 4: Essential Contract Law Review

1. a. Uniform Electronic Transactions Act.
2. c. Rescission
3. b. Revocation
4. d. cooling-period

5. c. counteroffer
6. a. Novation
7. b. terminates without the need for disaffirmation.
8. d. have to forfeit the earnest money deposit.
9. a. infeasibility.
10. c. The Statute of Frauds

Unit 5: Listing Agreements

1. c. Net listing
2. a. Open listing
3. b. not bound by fiduciary duties to either party.
4. d. net listing
5. b. exclusive right-to-sell
6. a. Exclusive right-to-represent

Unit 6: Purchase and Sale Contracts

1. d. It varies according to local custom.
2. a. Financing contingency
3. c. Forfeiture of buyer's deposit as liquidated damages
4. b. executory.
5. c. Negotiating period
6. a. equitable title.
7. b. sign and submit the Real Estate Offer Rejection Form within 48 hours.

Unit 7: Option-to-buy Contracts

1. b. Option-to-buy contract
2. a. equitable interest in
3. c. An option-to-buy places the optionee under no obligation to purchase the property.

Unit 8: Contracts for Deed

1. a. vendor
2. c. local contract law
3. b. Principal, interest, taxes and hazard insurance
4. d. Make the agreed upon periodic payments

Unit 9: Fiduciary Duties

1. b. Misrepresentation of expertise
2. a. Proper disclosure
3. c. Loyalty
4. d. environmental hazards.
5. a. Reasonable care and skill

Unit 10: Trust Fund Handling

1. c. Conversion
2. a. the lease expires or is terminated.
3. d. 5 years.
4. b. 48 hours of receipt.

Unit 11: Regulatory Compliance

1. b. Director of the Department of Labor, Licensing and Regulation
2. c. $10,000
3. a. an administrative law judge
4. b. Misrepresentation on a real estate license application
5. c. 90 days.

Unit 12: Professional Practices

1. b. Discrimination
2. a. The Americans with Disabilities Act
3. c. Equal Credit Opportunity Act
4. d. Duties to clients and customers
5. c. Pathways to Professionalism
6. a. Steering
7. d. Sherman Antitrust Act
8. b. Market allocation
9. c. Commitment to Excellence
10. a. Home Mortgage Disclosure Act
11. b. industry self-regulation through trade associations and institutes.
12. d. Respect for the Public, Respect for Property, and Respect for Peers
13. a. Tie-in agreement
14. c. Clayton Antitrust Act
15. b. Blockbusting

Unit 13: Measuring Real Property

1. a. Metes and bounds, rectangular survey system, and lot and block method
2. c. tier.
3. b. 640 acres
4. d. datums.
5. b. 5%
6. a. Metes and bounds
7. c. Rectangular survey system
8. d. meridians.
9. c. benchmarks
10. b. identification of the city, county, and state

Unit 14: Real Property Valuation

1. b.   Supply
2. a.   Utility
3. d.   Substitution
4. c.   deducted from the sale price of the comparable.
5. b.   contribution
6. a.   Desire
7. b.   the price mechanism.
8. b.   BPO
9. c.   Weighing the values indicated by adjusted comparables
10. a. Its market price

Unit 15: Essential Characteristics of Real Estate Investments

1. c.   Opportunity cost
2. c. $50,000
3. d.   Depreciation
4. b.   income property.
5. a.   The improvements

Unit 16: Investment Analysis of Non-income Property

1. c.   Sale price - costs of sale
2. b.   Appreciation
3. d.   adjusted basis.
4. a.   Beginning basis + capital improvements - exclusions
5. c.   two years.

Unit 17: Investment Analysis of Income Property

1. d.   cash reserve
2. b.   Deductions for depreciation are allowed on income properties.
3. a.   Gross operating income minus expenses and reserve allowances
4. c.   Principal and interest
5. a.   Depreciation

Unit 18: Investment Performance Analysis

1. b.   Income / price
2. a.   cash-on-cash return.
3. c.   She should divide the income by the rate of return.
4. b.   Return on investment
5. d.   net operating income / equity.

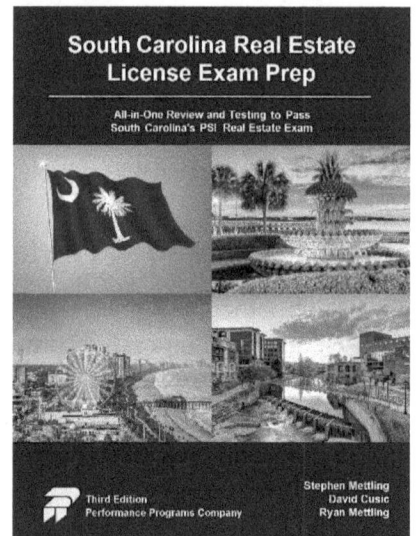

www.ingramcontent.com/pod-product-compliance
Lightning Source LLC
Chambersburg PA
CBHW080539220326

41599CB00032B/6312